1

AF	Air Force (part of DOD)
AFRL	Air Force Research Laboratory (part of AF/DOD)
CDC	Centers for Disease Control and Prevention (part of HHS)
CMS	Centers for Medicare & Medicaid Services (part of HHS)
DARPA	Defense Advanced Research Projects Agency (part of DOD)
DOC	Department of Commerce
DOD	Department of Defense
DOE	Department of Energy
DOL	Department of Labor
EPA	Environmental Protection Agency
EERE	Office of Energy Efficiency and Renewable Energy (part of DOE)
FDA	Food and Drug Administration
GSA	General Services Administration
HHS	Department of Health and Human Services
NASA	National Aeronautics and Space Administration
NIBIB	National Institute of Biomedical Imaging and Bioengineering (part of NIH/HHS)
NIEHS	National Institute of Environmental Health Sciences (part of NIH/HHS)
NIST	National Institute of Standards and Technology (part of DOC)
NIH	National Institutes of Health (part of HHS)
NOAA	National Oceanic and Atmospheric Administration (part of DOC)
ODPHP	Office of Disease Prevention and Health Promotion (part of HHS)
OMB	Office of Management and Budget
ONC	Office of the National Coordinator for Health Information Technology (part of HHS)
OPM	Office of Personnel Management
OSTP	Office of Science and Technology Policy
SBA	Small Business Administration
USAID	U.S. Agency for International Development
USPTO	United States Patent and Trademark Office (part of DOC)

TABLE OF CONTENTS

On January 4, 2011, President Obama signed into the law the America COMPETES Reauthorization Act (COMPETES), granting all agencies broad authority to conduct prize competitions to spur innovation, solve tough problems, and advance their core missions.

Prizes have an established track record of spurring innovation in the private and philanthropic sectors. This report details examples of how well-designed prizes integrated into a broader innovation strategy have enabled Federal agencies to:

- Pay only for success and establish an ambitious goal without having to predict which team or approach is most likely to succeed;
- Reach beyond the "usual suspects" to increase the number of solvers tackling a problem and to identify novel approaches, without bearing high levels of risk;
- Bring out-of-discipline perspectives to bear; and
- Increase cost-effectiveness to maximize the return on taxpayer dollars.

The Obama Administration has taken important steps to make prizes a standard tool in every agency's toolbox. The September 2009 *Strategy for American Innovation*[1] recognized the potential for prizes to mobilize America's ingenuity to solve some of the Nation's most pressing challenges. In March 2010, the Office of Management and Budget (OMB) issued a formal policy framework[2] to guide agency leaders in using prizes to advance their core missions. In September 2010, the Administration launched Challenge.gov[3], a one-stop shop where entrepreneurs and citizen solvers can find public-sector prizes. By September 2012, Challenge.gov had featured more than 200 competitions from over 45 Federal agencies, departments, and bureaus.[4]

The prize authority in COMPETES supports this effort. By giving agencies a clear legal path, the legislation makes it dramatically easier for agencies to use prizes. By significantly expanding the authority of all Federal agencies to conduct prize competitions, the legislation enables agencies to pursue more ambitious prizes with robust incentives.

Since the signing of the Act in January 2011, the Administration has laid the policy and legal groundwork to take maximum advantage of the new prize authority in the years to come. Policy and legal staff in the Office of Science and Technology Policy (OSTP) and

---

[1] http://www.whitehouse.gov/innovation/strategy and
http://www.whitehouse.gov/sites/default/files/microsites/ostp/innovationstrategy-prizes.pdf
[2] http://www.whitehouse.gov/sites/default/files/omb/assets/memoranda_2010/m10-11.pdf
[3] http://www.challenge.gov/
[4] http://www.whitehouse.gov/blog/2012/09/05/challengegov-two-years-and-200-prizes-later

OMB jointly developed a Fact Sheet and Frequently Asked Questions memorandum[5], issued in August 2011, which provided guidance to help streamline implementation of the new, government-wide authority.

Agencies including the Department of Health and Human Services (HHS) and the Environmental Protection Agency (EPA) have established strategies and policies to further accelerate widespread use of the new prize authority granted to them through COMPETES. Some agencies, such as the National Aeronautics and Space Administration (NASA) and the U.S. Agency for International Development (USAID), have personnel dedicated to lead prize design and administration efforts at their agencies and to provide internal support to program managers interested in making use of prizes.

As many agencies expand their use of the authorities provided to them under COMPETES, some agencies have continued to administer prizes and challenges developed under other pre-existing authorities, including agency-specific authorities, grant-making authority, and procurement authority, such as that provided by the Federal Acquisition Regulation (FAR), adding additional lessons learned and best practices regarding the use of prizes and challenges.

In addition, as called for in Section 24(n) of the Act, the General Services Administration (GSA) launched in July 2011 a contract vehicle[6] to dramatically decrease the amount of time required for agencies to tap the private-sector expertise that is so critical to early success. In Fiscal Year 2012 (FY 2012), agencies initiated their use of this contract vehicle. Adding to the support for the use of prizes, a government-wide Center of Excellence, led by NASA, provided multiple agencies support for the full lifecycle of pilot prize competitions: from design, through implementation, to post-prize evaluation.

The authority provided in COMPETES led to significant new efforts applying prizes to national priority areas including energy, health, and employment. In FY 2012, 27 prizes were conducted under this authority, compared to seven conducted from January-September 2011. Seven agencies including EPA, Department of Commerce (DOC), Department of Energy (DOE), Department of Health and Human Services (HHS), Department of Labor (DOL), Department of State, and the Small Business Administration (SBA) each launched prizes in FY 2012 enabled by the COMPETES authority. This look at the expanded use of the COMPETES prize authority in FY 2012, the first full fiscal year of

---

[5] https://cio.gov/wp-content/uploads/downloads/2012/09/Prize_Authority_in_the_America_COMPETES_Reauthorization_Act.pdf

[6] http://www.gsaelibrary.gsa.gov/ElibMain/sinDetails.do?scheduleNumber=541&specialItemNumber=541+4G&executeQuery=YES

implementation of that authority, indicates the ways this authority will continue to help agencies across the Federal government reap the benefits of high-impact prizes.

INTRODUCTION

From the 1714 Longitude Prize that stimulated the development of the world's first practical method to determine a ship's longitude, to the Orteig Prize that inspired Charles Lindbergh to fly nonstop from New York to Paris, to the 2011 Oil Cleanup X Challenge[7] awarded to a company from Illinois that demonstrated more than four times the previous best tested recovery rate for cleaning up oil from the ocean's surface, prizes have a long record of spurring innovation. A 2009 McKinsey report found that philanthropic and private-sector investment in prizes increased significantly in recent years, including $250 million in new prize money between 2000 and 2007.[8] Some of these incentive prizes included the GoldCorp Challenge[9], the Ansari X Prize[10], the Netflix Prize[11], and the Heritage Health Prize Competition[12].

Inspired by the success of philanthropic and private-sector prizes, the Obama Administration has taken important steps to accelerate public-sector adoption of these innovative tools. The *Strategy for American Innovation* recognized the potential for prizes and challenges to harness America's ingenuity to solve some of the Nation's most pressing challenges.[13] In March 2010, OMB issued a memorandum that provided a policy framework to guide agency leaders in using prizes to advance core missions.[14] In September 2010, the Administration launched Challenge.gov, a one-stop shop where entrepreneurs and citizen solvers can find and engage with public-sector prizes. By September 2012, the site had hosted over 200 challenges posted by more than 45 departments and agencies. By that point, more than 16,000 citizen "solvers" had participated in these competitions directly on Challenge.gov, with additional entrants joining the competitions through other sources.[15]

---

[7] http://www.iprizecleanoceans.org/

[8] McKinsey & Company, *"And the Winner Is..."; Capturing the promise of philanthropic prizes,* 2009, http://www.mckinseyonsociety.com/downloads/reports/Social-Innovation/And_the_winner_is.pdf

[9] Fast Company, http://www.fastcompany.com/magazine/59/mcewen.html

[10] http://space.xprize.org/ansari-x-prize

[11] http://www.netflixprize.com/

[12] http://www.heritagehealthprize.com/c/hhp

[13] http://www.whitehouse.gov/innovation/strategy
http://www.whitehouse.gov/sites/default/files/microsites/ostp/innovationstrategy-prizes.pdf

[14] http://www.whitehouse.gov/sites/default/files/omb/assets/memoranda_2010/m10-11.pdf

[15] http://www.whitehouse.gov/blog/2012/09/05/challengegov-two-years-and-200-prizes-later

On January 4, 2011, President Obama signed Public Law 111-358, the America COMPETES Reauthorization Act. Section 105 of this Act added section 24 (Prize Competitions) to the Stevenson-Wydler Technology Innovation Act of 1980 to provide all agencies broad authority to conduct prize competitions in order to spur innovation, solve tough problems, and advance their core missions. By giving agencies a simple and clear legal path, the Act supports the Administration's effort to make prizes a standard tool in every Federal agency's toolbox.

The Act also requires OSTP to annually submit to the Committee on Commerce, Science, and Transportation of the Senate and the Committee on Science and Technology of the House of Representatives a report on the activities carried out under the new prize authority during the preceding fiscal year.

This report documents the benefits the Federal government has already reaped from using incentive prizes, the steps the Administration has taken to establish a lasting foundation for use of the COMPETES prize authority, and detailed examples from FY 2012 of how the COMPETES prize authority is increasing the number of agencies that use prizes to achieve their missions more efficiently and effectively.

This scope of this report includes an overview of every prize conducted under the COMPETES prize authority in FY 2012 (as reported by Federal agencies to OSTP) and only selectively covers prizes conducted under other authorities available to agencies beyond the authority provided to agencies within COMPETES.

1. BENEFITS OF PRIZES IN THE PUBLIC SECTOR

The unique benefits of prizes have been well documented in the private and philanthropic sectors.[16] Early adopters in the public sector have begun to reap the rewards of well-designed prizes over the last several years. For example, NASA's Chief Technologist Mason Peck reports that "NASA recognizes the extraordinary opportunity that prize competitions represent: that they can inspire the development of transformative technologies by offering a means to engage with non-traditional sources of innovative ideas, all in a remarkably cost-effective way."[17] Specifically, prizes have enabled the Federal government to:

---

[16] *See e.g.*, McKinsey & Company, *"And the Winner Is..."; Capturing the promise of philanthropic prizes,* 2009, http://www.mckinseyonsociety.com/downloads/reports/Social-Innovation/And_the_winner_is.pdf

[17] NASA Report to Office of Science and Technology Policy on Prize Competitions for Fiscal Year 2012, submitted by Mason Peck, NASA Chief Technology Officer, to the Office of Science and Technology Policy, December 31, 2012

- **Pay only for success and establish an ambitious goal without having to predict which team or approach is most likely to succeed.** Contracts and grants are awarded based on proposals for future work, forcing agencies to assess merit based on past performance at the expense of disruptive innovation. With a focus on proven results, prizes empower new, untapped talent to deliver unexpected solutions to tough problems.

  For example, the $1.4 million Wendy Schmidt Oil Cleanup X Challenge,[18] which was awarded in October 2011 and supported by technical expertise from the Department of Interior and the National Oceanic and Atmospheric Administration (NOAA), inspired teams of entrepreneurs, engineers, and scientists worldwide to develop innovative, rapidly deployable, and highly efficient methods of cleaning up oil spills from the ocean surface. The winner, Elastec/American Marine – a growing Illinois-based manufacturer of oil spill and environmental equipment that uses local talent for nearly all its fabrication – recovered oil at a rate nearly four times the best previously recorded in controlled conditions. This significant advance, which involved grooved, high-surface-area spinning discs that grab large amounts of oil while leaving water behind, is all the more exciting given the potential for the novel mechanical solution to have a real impact on the industry. The competition judges were impressed by entrants' attention to real-world applications, ease of deployment, and consistency of performance in varied conditions. While the prize itself was privately funded, by bringing technical expertise to bear in the competition judging, the Department of Interior and NOAA advanced important shared goals, stimulated the development of new tools that can be brought to bear in future oil spills, and generated a treasure trove of data by testing novel technologies under controlled conditions.

- **Reach beyond the "usual suspects" to increase the number of solvers tackling a problem and to identify novel approaches, without bearing high levels of risk.** As Sun Microsystems co-founder Bill Joy once famously said, "No matter who you are, most of the smartest people work for someone else." Prizes are one tool to tap the top talent and best ideas wherever they lie, sourcing breakthroughs from a broad pool of both known and unknown sources of innovation in a given industry. As solutions are delivered prior to payment, the government can benefit from these novel approaches without bearing high levels of risk.

  In a survey of the nearly 3,000 solvers that competed in seven NASA prizes, 81% reported that they had never before responded to a government request for

---

[18] http://www.iprizecleanoceans.org/

proposals, let alone worked with NASA,[19] evidence of the expanded talent pool that prizes can attract.

In FY 2012, the U.S. Census Bureau conducted a prize competition[20] that challenged statisticians, mathematicians, and other data scientists to analyze Census data in order to create a statistical model to predict Decennial Census mail return rates at the Census block group level of geography. In order to improve the response rate in the future, Census planners need to develop appropriate strategies to gain the greatest amount of respondent cooperation for efficient data collection. The winning teams' models used statistical methods not previously utilized by the agency. As a result of the competition, the Census Bureau will pursue this promising technique. In addition, the challenge introduced the Census Planning Database to a new and diverse audience of data users, such as software engineers and university students focusing in information sciences and technology. The results of this prize competition will be used in modeling for the decennial census and demographic sample surveys.

- **Bring out-of-discipline perspectives to bear.** Empirical research conducted at the Harvard Business School has found that breakthrough solutions are most likely to come from outside the scientific discipline or at the intersection of two fields of study.[21]

Following the success of the Defense Advanced Research Projects Agency (DARPA) Urban Challenge that demonstrated dramatic leaps forward in the capabilities of autonomous vehicles, DARPA's Shredder Challenge called upon computer scientists and puzzle enthusiasts to compete for up to $50,000 by piecing together a series of shredded documents. The prize's goal was to identify and assess potential capabilities that could be used by U.S. warfighters operating in war zones, but that might also create vulnerabilities related to sensitive information that is protected through our own shredding practices throughout the U.S. national security community. Almost 9,000 teams registered to participate in DARPA's Shredder Challenge and 33 days after the challenge was announced, one small San Francisco-based team correctly solved the puzzles. The winning team spent nearly 600 person-hours developing algorithms and piecing together documents that were shredded into more than 10,000 pieces.

---

[19] http://www.nasa.gov/pdf/572344main_InnoCentive_NASA_PublicReport_2011-0422.pdf
[20] http://www.kaggle.com/c/us-census-challenge
[21] Jeppesen, Lars Bo, and Karim R. Lakhani. "Marginality and Problem-Solving Effectiveness in Broadcast Search." *Organization Science* 21 (September - October 2010): 1016-1033.

DARPA stated that experts had been skeptical that a solution could be produced at all, let alone in such a short time frame.[22]

- **Increase cost-effectiveness to maximize the return on taxpayer dollars.** As teams compete not just for the cash purse, but also for the associated validation, prestige, and satisfaction that results from solving important problems, prizes incent significant additional private-sector and philanthropic investment, leveraging the prize purse's impact. In the Orteig Prize won by Charles Lindbergh in 1927, nine teams spent a cumulative $400,000 to win the $25,000 prize purse.[23] More recently, the Ansari X PRIZE was won in 2004 by Burt Rutan and SpaceShipOne, after the 26 competing teams spent more than $100 million to win the prize.[24]

Prizes for open innovation offer these benefits, as well as numerous other advantages, such as the ability of prizes to inspire risk-taking by offering a level playing field through credible rules and robust judging mechanisms; to give entrepreneurs and innovators license to pursue an endorsed stretch goal that otherwise would have been considered overly audacious; and to establish clear success metrics and validation protocols that themselves become defining tools for the subject industry or field.

Of course, prizes are not the right tool for every problem. However, prizes can be a powerful mechanism if used strategically and systematically within an agency and when aligned with a broader strategy for spurring innovation and change. The COMPETES prize authority plays a critical role in unleashing that potential.

2. SUPPORT FOR SCALING THE USE OF PRIZES

Since 2009, the Obama Administration has taken important steps that are helping to scale the successful use of prizes and challenges across the entire Executive Branch. The COMPETES prize authority plays a critical role in the Administration's work to make prizes a standard tool in every agency's toolbox by granting clear, broad authority to all Federal agencies.

In FY 2012, Federal agencies were heterogeneous in their adoption of prizes as an open innovation tool. Some agencies, such as NASA (which continued operations of or newly

---

[22] www.darpa.mil/NewsEvents/Releases/2011/12/02_.aspx
[23] http://www.innovationinthecrowd.com/examples/orteig-prize.pdf
[24] http://space.xprize.org/ansari-x-prize

announced over a dozen prizes in FY 2012 under various authorities)[25], DOE, and Department of Defense (DOD) have a long track record of using prizes due to pre-existing agency authorities. Other agencies were early adopters of the COMPETES prize authority in FY 2011 and scaled these activities in FY 2012, such as HHS which scaled its prize activity from two prize programs under COMPETES authority in FY 2011 to 18 prizes under COMPETES authority in FY 2012.[26] Some agencies, such as the Census Bureau at DOC, offered their first prize in FY 2012, enabled by the COMPETES authority. Other agencies have yet to conduct a prize and are planning for prizes in future years.

The Administration has laid the policy and legal groundwork to take maximum advantage of the new authority in the years to come. Support for agencies in all stages of experience with prize design and administration includes:

- **Fact Sheet and Frequently Asked Questions:** Policy and legal staff in OSTP and OMB jointly developed a Fact Sheet and Frequently Asked Questions (FAQ) memorandum, which was issued in August 2011.[27] The Fact Sheet offered policy and programmatic staff a concise summary of the legislation's authorities and requirements and provided informal guidance to agencies in their implementation of the prize authority found in this legislation. To streamline and accelerate implementation of the new, government-wide authority, the FAQ addressed the questions most frequently raised by agency personnel, including general counsels, and thereby helped empower agencies to take advantage of the authorities in COMPETES, including the authority to conduct prizes up to $50 million with existing appropriations; to accept private sector funds for the design, administration, or prize purse of a competition; to partner with non-profits and tap the expertise of for-profits for successful implementation; and to co-sponsor with another agency.

- **Agency Implementation Guidance:** Following on the August 2011 Fact Sheet and FAQ, and through OSTP's support, agencies have begun to establish strategies and policies to further accelerate widespread use of the new prize authority granted to them under COMPETES. HHS has been at the forefront of agency

---

[25] NASA Report to Office of Science and Technology Policy on Prize Competitions for Fiscal Year 2012, submitted by Mason Peck, NASA Chief Technology Officer, to the Office of Science and Technology Policy, December 31, 2012

[26] HHS Reports on Prize Competition Activities Conducted in Fiscal Year 2012, submitted by Bryan Sivak, HHS Chief Technology Officer, and E.J. Holland Jr., HHS Assistant Secretary for Administration, to Dr. John P. Holdren, Director, Office of Science and Technology Policy, December 31, 2012

[27] *Prize Authority in the America COMPETES Reauthorization Act*: http://www.cio.gov/documents/Prize%20Authority%20in%20the%20America%20COMPETES%20Reauthorization%20Act.pdf

implementation efforts. On October 12, 2011, Secretary Sebelius issued a memorandum notifying the Department of the new COMPETES prize authority, outlining the strategy to optimize the use of prize competitions, and calling on the heads of operating and staff divisions to forecast their future use of prize competitions to stimulate innovation in advancing the agency's mission. The memorandum also highlighted the implementation framework established to accelerate the use of well-designed prizes. For example, Secretary Sebelius delegated the authority to conduct prize competitions to the Heads of all Operating and Staff Divisions. The Department also developed judging guidelines, governing principles outlining responsibilities for prize managers, a financial management policy for prize competitions, and a vehicle to share best practices across the Department. The full set of policy statements, guidance, and resources are available online. [28] Other agencies, including EPA, followed HHS's example in FY 2012, establishing agency-wide guidance for prizes conducted under the COMPETES authority.

Agencies such as NASA and USAID have dedicated personnel available to provide prize design and implementation assistance to other parts of the agency. For example, NASA reports that in FY 2012, the agency created and filled a new position, the Prizes and Challenges Program Executive within the Office of the Chief Technologist, to coordinate prize strategy for the Agency as a whole.[29] Additional agencies are now engaging actively in similar internal review and planning related to the prize authority granted under COMPETES.

- **General Services Administration Assistance:** Section 24(n) of COMPETES called on the GSA to "develop a contract vehicle to provide agencies relevant products and services, including technical assistance in structuring and conducting prize competitions to take maximum benefit of the marketplace as they identify and pursue prize competitions to further the policy objectives of the Federal Government." In response, GSA launched Sub-Schedule 541 4G, "Challenges and Competitions Services"[30] in July of 2011, thereby dramatically decreasing the amount of time required for agencies to tap the private sector expertise that is so critical to early success. To date, 15 contractors have joined Sub-Schedule 541 4G, offering agencies options for technical assistance, prize platforms, and communities of individuals and teams interested in entering prize competitions.

---

[28] http://www.hhs.gov/open/initiatives/challenges/

[29] NASA Report to Office of Science and Technology Policy on Prize Competitions for Fiscal Year 2012, submitted by Mason Peck, NASA Chief Technology Officer, to the Office of Science and Technology Policy, December 31, 2012

[30]

http://www.gsaelibrary.gsa.gov/ElibMain/sinDetails.do?scheduleNumber=541&specialItemNumber=541+4G&executeQuery=YES

In FY 2012, the Sub-Schedule was used for the first time by Federal agencies, with increased used planned for in Fiscal Year 2013 (FY 2013). GSA continues to inform private-sector vendors and agencies about the schedule and its benefits and assist agencies in taking advantage of the available services.

- **Government-wide Center of Excellence:** In 2011, the Administration launched a government-wide Center of Excellence for Collaborative Innovation (COECI) led by NASA to provide agencies guidance on all aspects of implementing prize competitions: from problem definition, to design of effective monetary and non-monetary incentives, to post-submission evaluation of solutions. From the Centennial Challenges Program, to the NASA Open Innovation Pavilion, to the NASA Tournament Lab, NASA is a public-sector leader with breadth and depth of experience and experimentation with prizes and challenges. Through COECI, NASA leverages that expertise across all NASA centers and directorates and helps other Federal agencies follow in its footsteps. For select agency pilots conducted through inter-agency agreements or through informal support, COECI leverages existing NASA open innovation infrastructure to provide a full suite of services — from prize design, through implementation, to post-prize evaluation — allowing agencies to rapidly experiment with these new methods before standing up their own capabilities. In addition, COECI captures and communicates best practices, case studies, and successful methodologies.

  In FY 2012, COECI executed Interagency Agreements with the U.S. Patent and Trademark Office (USPTO), HHS's Centers for Medicare and Medicaid Services (CMS), the Office of Personnel Management (OPM), and USAID. USPTO, CMS, and OPM launched application development challenges on the TopCoder platform using NASA's contract with Harvard University. USAID launched two idea generation challenges on the InnoCentive platform leveraging NASA's external crowdsourcing contract vehicle to advance their Tech Challenge for Atrocity Prevention,[31] a partnership with Humanity United. In addition, COECI also provided informal guidance to the Food and Drug Administration's (FDA) Center for Tobacco Products, DOE, and the National Institute of Standards and Technology (NIST), among other agencies.

- **Training and Capturing Best Practices:** OSTP, GSA, and COECI collaborated on a variety of training and educational activities in FY 2012 to assist a growing community practices of public-sector prize administrators to capture and share best practices and lessons learned in prize design and administration. GSA offers learning resources about prizes online at HowTo.gov.[32] OSTP, GSA, and COECI offered Federal agency prize administrators training events and webinars as well.

---

[31] http://thetechchallenge.org/
[32] http://www.howto.gov/challenges

For example, in June 2012, OSTP, the Case Foundation, the Joyce Foundation, and COECI co-hosted the *Collaborative Innovation* summit on the use of public-sector prizes to spur innovation in the Federal government. The cross-sector event brought together hundreds of Federal employees and their private-sector and philanthropic partners and counterparts and featured informative discussions with Administration officials, private-sector representatives, and Federal agencies that have conducted successful prize programs. The event resulted in a large amount of case studies and video resources available online.[33]

As agencies expanded their use of the clear and broad authorities provided to them under COMPETES in FY 2012, numerous public-sector prizes and challenges continued to be administered under other pre-existing authorities including agency-specific authorities; procurement authority such as that provided by the Federal Acquisition Regulation (FAR); the authority to award grants, participate in cooperative agreements, or both; and authority related to "necessary expense" doctrine, among others. These prizes add additional lessons learned and best practices to the growing community of practice engaged in public-sector prizes and challenges.

In FY 2013, as agencies complete their internal policies and strategies related to the implementation of programs under COMPETES; as more resources for related training of agency personnel and for the development, implementation, and promotion of challenges become available to agencies through GSA; and as COECI continues to provide support for pilot programs at other agencies, the use of the COMPETES prize authority will continue to increase, resulting in highly leveraged open innovation programs that help agencies address grand challenges and address needs in meeting their agency mission. Section 3 and Appendix 1 of this report will focus on the prizes developed under the specific prize authority provided by COMPETES. Appendix 2 will provide a brief summary of some prizes conducted under authorities, though this report is not comprehensive, as agency reporting to OSTP on prizes under authorities other than COMPETES is voluntary.

3. HIGHLIGHTS AND TRENDS FROM PRIZES CONDUCTED UNDER COMPETES IN FY 2012

Aided by the policy and legal framework and support for implementation of the new prize authority under COMPETES described in Section 2, agencies expanded their use of prizes conducted under that authority, with 27 prizes offered by seven agencies in FY 2012. These competitions provide evidence for how the COMPETES authority is helping agencies across the Federal government reap the benefits discussed earlier and to promote positive innovation and breakthroughs in national priority areas such as health,

---

[33] http://casefoundation.org/collaborative-innovation

energy, and employment. A summary of the highlights of FY 2012 activity under COMPETES is provided here.[34]

Driving Innovation in Health IT and Public Health Education

HHS emerged as a leader in implementing prize programs under the COMPETES authority in FY 2012, offering 18 prizes and challenges over the year. Four HHS agencies conducted prize competitions in FY2012, including the Centers for Disease Control and Prevention, National Institutes of Health, and Office of the Secretary. In HHS's FY 2012 report on use of COMPETES submitted to OSTP, HHS Chief Technology Officer Bryan Sivak and HHS Assistant Secretary for Administration E.J. Holland reported that these agencies found "prize competitions to be beneficial for advancing the mission of the agency and the primary objective of the challenge." HHS agencies made active use of the COMPETES authority to engage in partnerships to support prize funding and administration – in fact, 15 of the 18 FY 2012 competitions utilized partnerships with the private sector, academia, other federal agencies, or the non-profit sector to support aspects of the challenges, including publicity, funding and fundraising, technology and technical support, and subject matter expertise.

Investing in Innovation (i2)

The HHS Investing in Innovation (i2) initiative, announced in FY 2011, is a $5 million program to spur innovations in Health Information Technology (Health IT). Led by the Office of the National Coordinator for Health Information Technology (ONC), the core of the $5 million i2 program is a series of prize competitions – up to 15 each year – to accelerate innovation and adoption of Health Information Technology (Health IT) for improved clinical outcomes and efficient care delivery. ONC and its partners administered seven challenges through the i2 program in FY 2012.

My Air, My Health Challenge

One of the HHS ONC i2 challenges was conducted in partnership with the EPA and the National Institute of Environmental and Health Sciences (NIEHS): the "My Air, My Health Challenge."[35] Environment and public health are closely related and complementary fields — and their future depends on a closer understanding of those connections. New portable sensors have the potential to transform the way Federal agencies and the private sector measure and interpret the influence of pollution on health. These technologies can provide a picture that is detailed and personal, with dramatic implications for health care, air quality oversight, and individuals' control over their own environments and health. The EPA and HHS envision a future in which powerful,

---

[34] See the Appendix for a detailed account of all FY 2012 activities under COMPETES.
[35] https://www.innocentive.com/ar/challenge/9932947

affordable, and portable sensors provide a rich awareness of environmental quality, moment-to-moment physiological changes, and long-term health outcomes. Healthcare will be connected to the whole environment, improving diagnosis, treatment, and prevention at all levels. Many of the first steps toward this future have already been taken. Prototype projects have developed portable air quality and physiologic sensors, and experimental analysis tools for handling data that is higher in quantity, but often lower in quality, than more traditional monitoring techniques. The "My Air, My Health Challenge" was designed to build on this foundation. Challenge organizers sought solutions that integrate data from portable physiological and air quality monitors, producing a combined picture that is meaningful and usable.

The challenge was a multidisciplinary call to innovators and software developers to enable near real time, location-specific monitoring and reporting of air pollutants and potentially related physiological parameters, using a personal and portable integrated system to assess connections between the two. The system needed to link air-pollutant concentrations with physiological data, provide geo-coded and time-stamped files in an easy-to-use format, and transmit this data via existing networks to a central data repository provided by EPA and HHS.

The challenge was an integral part of the joint effort by HHS and EPA to find next-generation solutions in the area of environmental and health sensor technologies and exploring the interaction of environment and health through granular, near-real-time data collection. Grants or contracts were not appropriate because the agencies sought a variety of different ideas rather than having to select one approach based only on a proposal. In addition, the challenge afforded opportunities to communicate both agencies' interest in this topic to encourage private-sector research and development.

Phase 1 of the competition was still open as of the close of FY 2012. Full competition results will be reported in the FY 2013 report to Congress. The challenge stimulated interest in the topic from a wide range of individuals and institutions including large companies, universities, athletics suppliers, and lone innovators. This demonstrates that the challenge mechanism is a viable platform for agency collaboration around a topic of mutual interest. The creation of the actual prototypes based on the finalists' proposals will be a key component in evaluating the success of the challenge.

Reducing Hospital Readmissions for Patients

Another ONC i2 challenge[36] asked software developers to create an easy-to-use web-based tool to make post-discharge follow-up appointment scheduling an effective process for care providers, patients, and caregivers. Nearly one in five patients from a

---

[36] http://www.health2con.com/devchallenge/discharge-follow-up-appointment-challenge/

hospital will be readmitted within 30 days. A large proportion of readmissions can be prevented by improving communications and coordinating care before and after discharge from the hospital.

Research has shown that scheduling follow-up appointments and post-discharge testing before a patient is discharged is one of the critical elements of a safe and effective transition. Most patients across the country continue to leave the hospital without confirmed appointments and many providers remain frustrated by a highly manual and unreliable system. A growing number of innovative consumer-facing tools are becoming available for patients and care givers to schedule appointments and rate providers. However, these tools have not yet reached high levels of adoption within communities, and to date have not targeted the appointment scheduling needs of patients, caregivers, and providers at the point of discharge from a hospital.

Entrants to the challenge were asked to integrate inpatient data effectively and provide structured support for self-care; integrate design and usability concepts to drive patient and provider adoption and engagement; demonstrate innovative uses of mobile technologies; and demonstrate potential to improve health outcomes.

Entrants submitted numerous new easy-to-use tools[37] that have the potential to reduce patient readmissions through effective appointment scheduling, leading to improved patient health and reduced health care costs. The top submissions included easy-to-use, synchronized scheduling tools for providers, consumers, and caretakers while also providing assorted other functionalities that appeal to different types of stakeholders, including integration with multi-purpose patient portals, appointment transportation coordination, and automated reminders. The winning application, MyHealthDIRECT, is a web-based solution that effectively matches the demand for health care appointments with a supply of actual appointment slots.

Engaging Citizen Solvers in Energy Challenges

DOE offered several competitions in FY 2012 that challenged citizens and business to create innovative new solutions to clean energy challenges.

Apps for Energy

DOE's Apps for Energy competition offered $100,000 in prizes to software developers for the best new applications (apps) that help utility customers make the most out of their Green Button electricity usage data. Green Button is an open standard for sharing electricity data that is available to millions of utility customers, and combining Green Button data with other public data sources can help homeowners and businesses take

---

[37] http://www.health2con.com/devchallenge/discharge-follow-up-appointment-challenge/

action, understand energy usage, and make better-informed decisions. This competition sought to inspire innovative use of Green Button data, and a prize allowed DOE to leverage private-sector effort without predefining or limiting the solution set. Additionally, competitions have an existing following among the community of independent software developers, a key target community for DOE's goal of creating an active energy–focused developer community. Finally, the competition provided an opportunity to raise awareness of the existence and value of Green Button data.

The competition resulted in more than 50 submissions, and the discussion boards on Challenge.gov were heavily used during the competition, both indications of the beginning of an active developer community. Additionally, the winning apps show three diverse and valuable approaches to using Green Button data and two of the three top apps have either been used to found a company or have since been acquired by another company. An established company that was making its first foray into using Green Button data submitted the third app. The competition itself attracted over 12,000 followers.

DOE challenge organizers partnered formally with private-sector companies GRID21, PG&E, and Itron to sponsor the prize purse. These partners provided monetary and marketing and outreach support. Challenge organizers partnered informally with a great number of organizations to improve their outreach abilities, including the App Developers Alliance, Code for America, Innocentive, EPA, DOC, and various educational organizations.

SunShot Prize: Race to the Rooftops

In September 2012, DOE launched an audacious new market stimulation prize in support of the goals of its SunShot Grand Challenge, which aims to make solar competitive with fossil fuels by the end of the decade. The $10 million SunShot Prize[38] challenges the ingenuity of America's businesses and communities to make it faster, easier, and cheaper to install rooftop solar energy systems. Successful competitors will deploy at least 6,000 new rooftop photovoltaic installations in the U.S. at an average pre-subsidy non-hardware cost of $1 per watt. Winners will break this significant price barrier, considered to be unachievable a decade ago, and prove that they can repeatedly achieve a $1 per watt non-hardware cost using innovative, verifiable processes and business practices. The winners of the first phase of the competition will be announced in FY 2015 with cash awards likely to be made in 2016.

Despite unprecedented cost reductions for solar hardware over recent years, the total price to install and commission residential and small-commercial scale solar energy systems remains high. Designing and implementing practices that enable dramatic

---

[38] http://challenge.gov/DOE/410-sunshot-prize

reductions in the associated non-hardware costs of solar is now the greatest challenge to achieving national targets for attaining cost-competitive solar by 2020.

DOE has three main goals for Race to the Rooftops challenge:

- *Affordability*: Improve the affordability of residential and small commercial rooftop solar systems by breaking a significant price barrier for non-hardware costs, considered impossible a decade ago. Hardware costs have fallen more than 75% since 2008, the non-hardware costs have not made as significant of an advance. The goal of this prize is to help the community achieve lower all in costs to the consumer by cutting through much of the red tape.

- *Solar Market Maturity*: Inspire U.S. businesses and communities to create the right market conditions for growth and job creation.

- *Subsidy Independence*: Help the private sector transition to post-subsidy market while maintaining strong growth and resilience.

DOE has partnered formally with the College of Nanoscale Science and Engineering at State University of New York at Albany, to promote and provide ongoing outreach activities for the prize. Based on the feedback, inquires, and comments received to date, challenge organizers think there is a great interest in the solar community in this new market stimulation prize.

New Solutions for Entrepreneurs, Job-Seekers, and Small Businesses

DOL and SBA offered competitions to create applications that would leverage open government data and benefit entrepreneurs, job-seekers, and small businesses. Two apps challenges from DOL are summarized here.

Equal Pay App Challenge

Through the Equal Pay App Challenge, the National Equal Pay Task Force and DOL engaged innovators, educators, and IT developers to help build innovative tools to educate the public about the gender pay gap and promote equal pay for women. Nearly 50 years after President Kennedy signed the Equal Pay Act, women are still paid less than their male counterparts for doing comparable jobs. This pay gap means that each time the average woman starts a new job, she is likely to start from a lower base salary, and that, over time, the pay gap between her and her male colleagues is likely to grow. For the average working woman, the pay gap means she will receive $150 less in her weekly paycheck, $8,000 less at the end of the year, and $380,000 less over her lifetime. For women of color and women with disabilities, the disparity is even bigger.

Through the challenge, DOL engaged leaders in academia, non-profit organizations, industry innovators, IT professionals, and other equal pay supporters to use publicly available labor data and other online resources to educate users about the pay gap and develop tools to promote equal pay. DOL's four primary goals were to provide greater access to pay data by gender, race, and ethnicity; provide tools for early career coaching; improve education on negotiation; and promote online mentoring. Private sector partners for the challenge included Women Innovate Mobile, Carnegie Mellon University, Google, The Daily Muse, Salary.com, Interview Street, and the Massachusetts Institute of Technology (MIT).

The Equal Pay App Challenge on Challenge.gov advanced DOL's mission by leveraging existing program information, technology, and public innovation to raise awareness on equal pay and provide effective tools for employers and employees. The competition amplified the Equal Pay Taskforce's mission on wage equality by expanding the amount of quality online tools, effective messaging, and partnerships with non-traditional stakeholders in the academic and digital spectrum. The competition was featured on multiple media outlets including Forbes, The Daily Muse, New York Times, and Sacramento Bee, in addition to other online publications and mainstream blogs.

Disability Employment App Challenge

This challenge asked developers to help build innovative tools to improve employment opportunities and outcomes for people with disabilities. Nearly twenty-two years after the passage of the Americans with Disabilities Act and thirty-nine years after the passage of the Rehabilitation Act of 1973 – two of the most significant disability employment-related pieces of legislation in American history – people with disabilities continue to be employed at much lower levels than the general population. Not only do people with disabilities have a significantly higher unemployment rate than the general population, they also have a much lower labor force participation rate. For minorities with disabilities, these disparities are even greater. This represents a significant loss of willing and able talent to the American workforce, loss of income for people without jobs, and economic loss to the country. In this challenge, DOL leveraged technology in innovative ways to promote recruitment resources for employers, develop job-training and skill-building tools for job seekers, facilitate employment-related transportation options, and expand web and Information Communication Technology accessibility.

Three category prizes were awarded for innovation, public voting, and accessibility:

- *Innovation Award Winner*: Access Jobs is a job search portal specifically designed for job seekers with disabilities. The website implements usable accessibility techniques, such as responsive design, which allow the website to be experienced in the same way across all platforms.

- *The People's Choice Award Winner*: VoisPal is an Android-based app designed to help people with speech difficulties.

- *Above and Beyond Accessibility Award Winner*: Accelerated Dynamic Content: (AccDC) is a scalable, cross-browser, and cross-platform compatible Dynamic Content Management System that automates the rendering of dynamic content to ensure accessibility for screen reader and keyboard-only users.

CONCLUSION

Prizes have an impressive track record of spurring innovation in the private and philanthropic sectors. More than 45 Federal agencies, departments, and bureaus conducted over 200 prizes by September 2012, including 27 competitions conducted by seven agencies under the COMPETES prize authority in FY 2012. These agencies have reaped the rewards of well-designed prizes integrated into a broader innovation strategy. The successes of these public-sector prizes show what can be expected from more Federal agencies as they develop the expertise and capacity to use prizes strategically and systematically to advance their core mission.

The COMPETES prize authority is a critical step toward making prizes a standard tool in every agency's toolbox. By expanding the authority of all Federal agencies to conduct prize competitions and by giving agencies a clear legal path, the legislation makes it easier for agencies to use prizes and enables agencies to pursue more ambitious prizes with robust incentives.

The Administration has laid the policy and legal groundwork for agencies to continue to take advantage of the new prize authority in the years to come and has set up support for agencies, such as training events and resources, GSA's contact vehicle that decreases the amount of time required for agencies to tap private sector expertise, and the government-wide Center of Excellence for Collaborative Innovation through which NASA supports the design and implementation of pilot prize programs for other Federal agencies. A number of agencies have begun to establish specific strategies and policies to further accelerate widespread use of the COMPETES prize authority throughout their organization.

As the Administration expands the foundation of support for the widespread use of the COMPETES prize authority, prizes conducted under the authority unleashed significant new activity in national priority areas such as energy, health, and employment. Continued and increased use of the authority in the years to come will allow agencies across the Federal government to reap the benefits of high-impact prizes for open innovation in the years to come.

APPENDIX 1: AGENCY PROGRAMS CONDUCTED UNDER THE AMERICA COMPETES REAUTHORIZATION ACT OF 2010

This Appendix provides a complete summary of all prizes and challenges conducted in FY 2012 under the prize authority provided to agencies in COMPETES and does not include any of the multiple prize competitions conducted under other authorities in FY 2012 or prior.

LIST OF CHALLENGES

1. **Department of Commerce**
   - 1.1. Census Return Rate Challenge

2. **Department of Energy**
   - 2.1. National Clean Energy Business Plan Competition
   - 2.2. Apps for Energy
   - 2.3. SunShot Prize

3. **Environmental Protection Agency and Department of Health and Human Services**
   - 3.1. My Air, My Health Challenge

4. **Department of Health and Human Services**
   - 4.1. SMART-Indivo Challenge
   - 4.2. EHR Accessibility Module Challenge
   - 4.3. Discharge Follow-up Appointment Challenge
   - 4.4. Reporting Patient Safety Events Challenge
   - 4.5. popHealth Tool Development Challenge
   - 4.6. One in a Million Hearts Challenge
   - 4.7. What's in your Health Record Video Challenge
   - 4.8. Managing Meds Video Challenge
   - 4.9. Healthy People 2020 Leading Health Indicators App Challenge
   - 4.10. Beat Down Blood Pressure Video Challenge
   - 4.11. Health New Year Challenge
   - 4.12. Design by Biomedical Undergraduate Teams (Debut) Challenge
   - 4.13. Now Trending: #Health in My Community
   - 4.14. 2012 Surgeon General's Video Contest: Tobacco – I'm Not Buying It
   - 4.15. Surgeon General's Healthy Apps Challenge
   - 4.16. Seeing My World Through a Safer Lens Video Challenge
   - 4.17. Million Hearts Caregiver Video Challenge

5. **Department of Labor**
   - 5.1. Equal Pay App Challenge
   - 5.2. Disability Employment App Challenge

DETAILED CHALLENGE REPORTS

1. **Department of Commerce**

   1.1. Census Return Rate Challenge

Overview: The U.S. Census Bureau conducted a prize competition that challenged statisticians, mathematicians, and other data scientists to analyze Census data in order to create a statistical model to predict Decennial Census mail return rates at the Census block group level of geography. In order to improve the response rate in the future, Census planners need to develop appropriate strategies to gain the greatest amount of respondent cooperation for efficient data collection. The results of this prize will be used in modeling for the decennial census and demographic sample surveys.

Website:
http://www.kaggle.com/c/us-census-challenge

Problem Statement: Over the last two decades, the Census Bureau has seen a decline in cooperation rates with Decennial Censuses and ongoing surveys. The Census Bureau conducted a prize competition capitalizing on the expertise of data scientists to improve upon or provide different methodologies in creating a predictive statistical model on Census mail return rates that help the agency plan and design more efficient Censuses and surveys. The Census Bureau provided participants with a public use statistical dataset comprised of 2010 Census and the 5-year American Community Survey estimates (the Census Planning Database). To succeed, models had to be successful, it must have maintained accuracy in its predictions when tested by officials with a validation dataset that was not available to the participants.

Goal: The competition's primary objective was to obtain a better statistical model for predicting return rates at the block group level. This predictive model aids Census planners in better developing and improving upon strategies to contact and gain respondent coordination for timely and efficient data collection.

Why a Prize as Preferred Method: The Census Bureau chose to conduct a prize competition instead of utilizing other acquisition methods because the Kaggle online platform provided the Bureau with a large variety of data scientists that would have been difficult to tap through traditional contract, grant, or cooperative agreement approaches. Census wanted to move beyond the usual suspects and involve a large variety of data scientists with varying levels of expertise to maximize innovation and receive as many different methods and models as possible.

Participants: The competition targeted statisticians, mathematicians, and other data scientists experienced in dealing with large amounts of data and statistical models. Participation was open to all members of the Kaggle community who agreed to the terms and conditions set forth by the Census Bureau and Kaggle. There were 291 total participants. Of these participants, 244 were teams ranging in size from one to four members. Participants were located worldwide in countries including Australia, Czech Republic, and India, as well as throughout the United States.

Timeline: On August 31, 2012, the competition launched and remained open through November 1, 2012. A separate data visualization competition began on November 1, 2012 and lasted through November 11, 2012.

Solicitation and Outreach Methods and Results: Prior to the launch of the competition, the Census Bureau widely advertised the upcoming competition in order to mobilize potential participants. These efforts varied but included: Census Bureau personnel creating and distributing flyers at the Joint Statistical Meetings (JSM) of the American Statistical Association's annual conference in San Diego; announcing the competition at a JSM roundtable luncheon and an invited session; creating a specialized web page and slider on the Census Bureau public facing website; a public announcement in the Federal Register; and advertisement on the Kaggle website itself. The Census Bureau found these methods to be highly effective and was extremely pleased with the level of participation received. The Census Bureau will utilize these same solicitation and outreach methods in any similar, future outreach efforts.

Incentives: The total available prize money was $25,000 (first place $14,000, second place $7,500, third place $2,500, and data visualization competition $1,000).

Evaluation: The Kaggle website's Leaderboard kept track of each entrant's score and comparative rank based on the predicted results in the entry and ground truth of a validation dataset. At the close of the competition, scores were calculated from the predicted results and ground truth in the testing dataset. The Top 3 eligible entrants on the Private Leaderboard were declared as the prize winners.

Resources: A team of three people at Census oversaw the competition.

Results: The competition advanced the mission of the Census Bureau in several ways. First, the winning team's models used statistical methods not previously utilized by the agency. All three top models made use of a class of *voting* or *committee* method that fall under the heading of "Statistical Machine Learning" techniques. These methods have a very high profile in statistics and are typically applied in computer science. Census Bureau statisticians had not used this method before when modeling Census mail return rates andas a result of the competition, the Census Bureau will pursue this promising technique. Second, the challenge introduced the Census Planning Database to a new and diverse audience of data users, such as software engineers and university students focusing in information sciences and technology. Given these outcomes, challenge organizers consider the challenge to have been a success and plan to study and apply the winning model techniques and methods as they plan for Census 2020.

2. Department of Energy

2.1. National Clean Energy Business Plan Competition

Overview: The DOE's National Clean Energy Business Plan Competition (NCEBPC) is designed to build regional networks of student-focused business creation competitions across the country. Six regional organizations hold clean energy business plan competitions, and the competition culminates in the six regional winners competing for a National Grand Prize of $100,000.

Website:
http://techportal.eere.energy.gov/commercialization/natlbizplan.html

Problem Statement: The NCEBPC aims to inspire clean energy innovation across the country by creating businesses from best in-class technology research while inspiring and cultivating America's next generation of entrepreneurs to drive those businesses forward. Six regional DOE-funded business plan competitions send a finalist to Washington, D.C. to compete for the Grand Prize in DOE's National Competition. All business plan proposals must fall within DOE's Office of Energy Efficiency and Renewable Energy (EERE) mission and technology portfolio. DOE established guidelines that defined regional NCEBPC competitions. Regional competitions are encouraged to communicate and collaborate with other regional organizers in order expand network connections.

As a program whose goals include the development of the next generation of entrepreneurs, NCEBPC requires that students be highly involved in each competition's management and execution – at least 50% of any participating team's team members must be actively enrolled in an accredited U.S. university or college.
DOE promotes openness and transparency by requiring all competition entrants to disclose the status of all intellectual property (IP) used in the competitions. Competitions must demonstrate an effort to cultivate and recruit business plans based on technologies derived from U.S. universities or national labs. To ensure a level playing field among business plan teams nationwide, all entrants must be early stage venture

investments and may not have equity capital totaling more than $200,000 prior to selection of regional winners. Student members of the formal team must have combined minimum equity of 20% of the company.

Goal: The DOE has created the NCEBPC and funded the regional competitions with several goals in mind:
- Inspire students to engage in clean energy entrepreneurship.
- Build regional networks through the competitions that create linkages between technologists, academics, and investors.
- Enable the launch of innovative cleantech startups by providing seed funding and in-kind services to young entrepreneurs.
- Advance clean energy technologies by engaging students, innovators, and technologists to bring innovative technologies to market.

Why a Prize as Preferred Method: The NCEBPC seeks to bridge the investor, technology, and academic communities by inspiring cleantech entrepreneurship in students. By working with the private sector, through in-kind sponsorships, cash prizes, and having the business and investor community serve as judges and mentors, the competition brings together the communities in a way that could not be done through a grant alone. The DOE funded the regional competitions through a competitive grant solicitation; however, each region must raise funds on their own to support the competitions. The National Grand Prize, however, is solely funded by private-sector partners. The final national phase brings together the regions.

Participants: The NCEBPC's primary target audience is graduate and undergraduate students in U.S. universities and colleges. The competition, through its six regions, received 299 eligible submissions from teams in its first year. The six regional winners participated in the National portion of the competition. Teams must go through the regional competition process in order to compete in the National Grand Prize.

Timeline: The NCEBPC was launched in 2011, with the inaugural competition taking place in June of 2012. The grant is for three years for the regions; however, each region must make their competition sustainable beyond the grant period. The DOE aims to make the NCEBPC an annual event beyond 2014. For the applications, each regional competition sets its own deadlines. Most of the applications are due between late December and early March. Each competition must hold their final round of selection for their winner by early May. The National Competition takes place in June. The 2012 Competition took place June 11-13, 2012 in Washington, DC.

Solicitation and Outreach Methods and Results: The NCEBPC utilized many forms of media to disseminate information about the prize. These included social media, traditional press, http://energy.gov/ through the EERE and Secretary's blog, and Challenge.gov. Each of the regions has their own outreach strategy as well. The DOE will be pairing up with more associations and other groups to disseminate information about the National and regional competitions.

Incentives: The National Competition incentive is a $100,000 prize, provided by Wells Fargo. For the 2012 Competition, the cash prize was distributed to the winning team through the Clean Energy Alliance (CEA); the funds were not transferred to or through DOE. Other prizes for the 2012 Competition included technical, analytical, and business support selected and offered to help the teams after the competition to help them connect to the investor communities, providing legal and advisory services, and give them resources to expose their technology to the greater cleantech community. These resources and services included:

- Technical and commercialization support provided by the National Renewable Energy Laboratory (NREL)
- Access and office space at NREL's Colorado Center for Renewable Energy Economic Development (CREED)
- Access to NREL's Venture Capital Advisory Network
- Advisory services from Battelle Ventures tailored to specific technology and business needs
- Technical and commercialization assistance provided by one of CEA's 18 incubators depending on individual business needs, and geography
- Participation in the NREL Industry Growth Forum and The Cleantech Open
- Profile of technology and business case on EERE's Energy Innovation Portal

Evaluation: While the regions can determine their own judging criteria, the National Competition adheres to these judging criteria:

- Solutions/Products (30%): (1) the value a solution/product can deliver to customers, (2) clear and convincing description of the market differentiation for the solution, and (3) technical feasibility.
- Go-To-Market Plan (30%): (1) ability to demonstrate evidence of customer valuation/validation, (2) prove to the best of their ability that the business is scalable.
- Team Plan (20%): (1) how well the team is positioned to successfully carry out their business plans, (2) commitment to enterprise, and (3) gaps that currently exist in the organization and action plan to fill the gaps.
- Impact on EERE Mission (20%): (1) how the solution/product will strengthen the economy, protect the environment, and reduce dependence on foreign oil; and (2) identification of which of the eleven areas of EERE's mission space will benefit from the solution/product: Renewable Energy (Solar, Wind, Water, Biomass, Geothermal, Hydrogen and Fuel Cells) and Energy Efficiency (Homes, Buildings, Vehicles, Manufacturing, and Government).

Partnerships: The U.S. DOE NCEBPC partnered formally with Wells Fargo, NREL, Mintz Levin & ML Strategies, the Clean Energy Alliance (CEA), Battelle Ventures, Cleanlaunch, and The Cleantech Open. Additionally, their Federal partners included the DOC and OSTP.

Resources: No other DOE appropriations were used for the National Competition. The regional competitions are a $2.1M 3-year competitive grant program.

Results: The NCEBPC engaged multiple stakeholders at both the national and the regional level. More than 300 teams were involved in 2012 NCEBPC, with more than 250+ attendees at the national event. As a result of the competition, as of November 2012, reported metrics include:
- More than 52 startups incorporated
- 55 patents and disclosures have been filed
- 31+ FTEs created

2.2. Apps for Energy

Overview: DOE's Apps for Energy offered $100,000 to software developers for the best new apps that help the public make the most of Green Button electricity usage data.

Website:
http://appsforenergy.challenge.gov/

Problem Statement: DOE's Apps for Energy competition offered $100,000 in prizes to software developers for the best new apps that help utility customers make the most out of their Green Button[39] electricity usage data. Green Button is an open standard for sharing electricity data that is available to millions of utility customers, and combining Green Button data with other public data sources can help homeowners and businesses take action, understand energy usage, and make better-informed decisions.

Goal: DOE had three goals for the Apps for Energy competition:
- Increase the value of Green Button data for residential and commercial utility customers by providing new tools for analyzing, viewing, reducing, and sharing their electricity usage
- Encourage the creation of innovative apps with commercial potential by individuals, startups, and small organizations
- Create an active and energy-focused developer community

Why a Prize as Preferred Method: This competition sought to inspire innovative use of Green Button data, and a prize allowed DOE to leverage private-sector effort without predefining the types of applications DOE would like to see. Additionally, competitions have an existing following among the community of independent software developers, a

---

[39] http://collaborate.nist.gov/twiki-sggrid/bin/view/SmartGrid/GreenButtonInitiative

key target community for DOE's goal of creating an active energy–focused developer community. Finally, the competition itself provided an opportunity to raise awareness of the existence and value of Green Button data.

Participants: The primary target audiences were developers who are not already engaged in the energy sector and developers who are engaged in the energy sector but are not familiar with the Green Button format. The competition received 56 eligible submissions from individuals, small teams, and large organizations. Small teams were the most common, followed by individual entries.

Timeline:
Submission Period Began: April 5, 2012
Submission Period Ended: May 15, 2012
Judging Began: May 17, 2012
Judging Ended: May 21, 2012
Public Voting Ended: May 31, 2012

Solicitation and Outreach Methods and Results: Challenge organizers used an extensive public engagement campaign focused on targeted outreach to prominent tech and energy influencers on Twitter, as well as on Facebook to a lesser extent. Challenge organizers also managed to get a number of stories about the competition in online technology and energy press. Energy.gov and Challenge.gov were used as hubs for frequent competition updates and active support, so that competition followers were more likely to submit high quality work. Finally, challenge organizers worked with a number of professional organizations to alert their memberships.

Incentives: The primary incentive was $100,000 in prize money. $50,000 was provided by the Office for Electricity and Energy Reliability and $25,000 was provided each by PG&E and Itron. For the non-monetary incentives, each winner was included in the 2012 Energy Datapalooza event and their app was featured on Energy.gov.

Evaluation: The judging panel consisted of experts and managers from DOE, the sponsoring organizations, other Federal agencies, and the software design and development industry, and selected the Best Overall App and Student Award based upon the following criteria:
- *Impact:* Strength of the submission's potential to help individuals, organizations, and communities make informed decisions about their electricity use.
- *Creativity and Innovation:* Degree of new thinking the submission brings to applications for the energy sector, and the creativity shown in designing for impact.
- *Implementation:* The submission's user experience and interactive capabilities, with preference given to applications that are easily accessible to a range of consumers, including those with disabilities.

A preliminary panel of judges selected by DOE initially screened submissions. The preliminary panel conducted an initial screening of the apps for eligibility and verified that the apps worked as advertised in the descriptions. The finalists were then passed to the judges for ranking. Each judge ranked the apps independently and the rankings were combined to determine the winner.

Partnerships: Challenge organizers partnered formally with GRID21, PG&E, and Itron to sponsor the prize. They provided monetary and marketing and outreach support. Challenge organizers partnered informally with a great number of organizations to improve their outreach abilities, including the App Developers Alliance, Code for America, Innocentive, EPA, DOC, and various educational organizations.

Resources: In addition to the prize money, the competition required $2,000 in additional funding, used to customize the website and employ ChallengePost to vet the validity of users participating in the Popular Choice Award vote.

Results: The competition resulted in a large number of submissions, and the discussion boards on Challenge.gov were heavily used during the competition, both indications of the beginning of an active developer community. Additionally, the winning apps show 3 diverse and valuable approaches to using Green Button data and 2 of the 3 top apps have either been used to found a company or have since been acquired by another company. An established company that was making its first foray into using Green Button data submitted the third app. The competition itself attracted over 12,000 followers.

2.3. SunShot Prize: Race to the Rooftops

Overview: DOE's $10 million SunShot Prize challenges the ingenuity of America's businesses and communities to make it faster, easier, and cheaper to install rooftop solar energy systems. Successful competitors will deploy domestically and in two phases, at least 6,000 new rooftop photovoltaic installations at an average pre-subsidy non-hardware cost of $1 per watt. Winners will break this significant price barrier, considered to be unachievable a decade ago, and prove that they can repeatedly achieve a $1 per watt non-hardware cost using innovative, verifiable processes and business practices.

Website:
http://challenge.gov/DOE/410-sunshot-prize

Problem Statement: Despite unprecedented cost reductions for solar hardware over recent years, the total price to install and commission residential and small-commercial scale solar energy systems remains high. Designing and implementing practices that enable reductions in the associated non-hardware costs of solar is now the greatest challenge to achieving national targets for attaining cost-competitive solar by 2020.

Goal: DOE has three main goals for Race to the Rooftops challenge:

- *Affordability*: Improve the affordability of residential and small commercial rooftop solar systems by breaking a significant price barrier for non-hardware costs, considered impossible a decade ago. Hardware costs have fallen more than 75% since 2008, the non-hardware costs have not made as significant of an advance. The goal of this prize is to help the community achieve lower all in costs to the consumer by cutting through much of the red tape.
- *Solar Market Maturity*: Inspire U.S. businesses and communities to create the right market conditions for growth and job creation.
- *Subsidy Independence*: Help the private sector transition to post-subsidy market while maintaining strong growth and resilience.

Why a Prize as Preferred Method: The SunShot Prize not only rewards for results in cost effective ways, it increases the number and the diversity of individuals, organizations, and teams that are addressing this problem. In addition, DOE expects the industry overall to invent and deploy new business concepts and models during a period of two years. This will help all market players, not only the best, to participate, excel, and improve while focusing on their core value proposition to end consumers.

Participants: The target audiences are teams consisting of numerous organizations such as solar developers, installers (large and small), state and local governments, utilities, property owners/managers, new housing builders, home service providers, trade associations, and new market entrants. The prize is open to all U.S. citizens or permanent residents and to all public and private organizations such as a private or publicly traded company or an institution of higher education, an association, or other nonprofit organization, that maintains the U.S. as a primary place of business.

Timeline:
Registration to compete period begins: 9/12/2012
Submission period begins: 12/31/2012
Registration to compete deadline: 10/31/2014
Pre-submission assessment period ends: 11/30/2014
Phase I Prize submission deadline: 12/31/2014
Phase II Prize submission deadline: 12 months after Phase I submission
Anticipated date for announcing Phase I winners: Summer 2015
Anticipated Date for awarding Phase II cash awards: Spring 2016

Solicitation and Outreach Methods and Results: Challenge organizers have been applying a targeted engagement campaign using webinars, email blasts, blog posts, and web updates that target tens of thousands of people and organizations. Challenge organizers also managed to get a number of press releases about the competition in online technology, media, and energy press. The SunShot Initiative website, Energy.gov, and Challenge.gov were used as hubs for frequent competition updates and active support to potential contenders. Challenge organizers have partnered with the College of Nanoscale Science and Engineering at State University of New York at Albany (CNSE), to promote and provide ongoing outreach through annual workshops dedicate to the SunShot Prize and its potential contenders.

Incentives: The primary incentive is a $10,000,000 total cash award given to three winning teams. In addition, winners will have rights to use the title "SunShot Prize Winner." The first team will have the rights to the title "SunShot Prize Winner of America's Most Affordable Rooftop Solar."

Evaluation: DOE will establish by 2014 an Evaluation Review Committee (ERC) composed of Federal and non-Federal subject matter experts, including third-party organizations, to review entries submitted under this competition and determine winners. In addition, DOE will use a third-party auditing firm to conduct extensive technical and financial evaluations in order to assist the ERC in making its selections. There are three main criteria in judging applications:

1. *Technical Field Assessment*: Examiners will review evidence of installation qualification and compliance with requirements. Examiners may conduct random on-site visits to verify submitted records by applicants.
2. *Financial and Accounting Assessment*: Examiners will perform a complete audit to determine financial propriety of submissions. Auditors will review all financial transactions, accounting procedures, internal controls, financial terms, and financial reporting systems.
3. *Business Sustainability*: Examiners will evaluate the sustainability of teams' business models to deploy solar in subsidy-free U.S. markets. Future installations must be feasible without subsidies or rebates at average non-hardware costs of $1/W or less.

Partnerships: Challenge organizers partnered formally with the College of Nanoscale Science and Engineering at State University of New York at Albany to promote and provide ongoing outreach activities.

Resources: In addition to the $10,000,000 prize money, the competition requires roughly $50,000 annually to fund and support outreach activities.

Results: DOE released the SunShot Prize: Race to the Rooftops in September 2012. Based on the feedback, inquires, and comments received through formal communication channels and based on the number webinar attendance, challenge organizers think there is a great interest in the solar community in this challenge.

3. Environmental Protection Agency and Department of Health and Human Services

3.1. My Air, My Health Challenge

Overview: Environment and public health are closely related and complementary fields—and their future depends on a closer understanding of those connections. New portable sensors have the potential to transform the way challenge organizers measure and interpret the influence of pollution on health. These technologies can provide a picture that is more detailed and more personal, with dramatic implications for health care, air quality oversight, and individuals' control over their own environments and health. The EPA and HHS — including NIEHS and ONC — envision a future in which powerful, affordable, and portable sensors provide a rich awareness of environmental quality, moment-to-moment physiological changes, and long-term health outcomes. Healthcare will be connected to the whole environment, improving diagnosis, treatment, and prevention at all levels. Many of the first steps toward this future have already been taken. Prototype projects have developed portable air quality and physiologic sensors, and experimental analysis tools for handling data that is higher in quantity, but often lower in quality, than more traditional monitoring techniques. The "My Air, My Health Challenge" was designed to build on this foundation. Challenge organizers sought solutions that integrate data from portable physiological and air quality monitors, producing a combined picture that is meaningful and usable.

Website:
https://www.innocentive.com/ar/challenge/9932947

Problem Statement: The challenge was a multidisciplinary call to innovators and software developers to enable near real time, location-specific monitoring and reporting of air pollutants and potentially related physiological parameters, using a personal/ portable integrated system to assess connections between the two. The system needed to link air-pollutant concentrations with physiological data, provide geo-coded and time-stamped files in an easy-to-use format, and transmit this data via existing networks to a central data repository provided by EPA and HHS.

Goal: The challenge was structured in 2 phases:

Phase 1 – Project Plan
In Phase 1, entrants needed to:
- Propose a plausible link between health outcomes and airborne pollutants (chemical species and/or particulates), and provide evidence to support a plausible and physiologically meaningful relationship between airborne pollutants and physiological metrics in a defined population.
- Propose a prototype design and development plan for an integrated multi-sensor and data management system that may be easily worn or carried by individuals within the defined target community/population.

- Conceptualize data generation, management (may include processing & on-board storage), and transmission functionality of the device.
- Propose a small-scale proof-of-concept study to validate the proposed prototype.
- Study design process must include input from the target community/population.

Phase 2 – Proof-of-Concept Pilot Project
- Finalists attended an event for feedback, questions, and business/entrepreneurial resources prepared by Challenge sponsors (EPA, HHS ONC, and NIEHS).
- Solvers developed prototypes and executed experimental validation of the system to bring together data from personal air quality and physiological monitors, showing how these types of data and sensors can be integrated for practical use by health and environmental agencies, and by individual citizens. Proof-of-concept data needed to illustrate the accuracy and precision of the raw data and of any processed data produced by the system.

Why a Prize as Preferred Method: The challenge was an integral part of the joint effort by HHS and EPA to find next-generation solutions in the area of environmental and health sensor technologies and exploring the interaction of environment and health through granular, near-real-time data collection. Grants or contracts were not appropriate because the agencies sought a variety of different ideas rather than having to select one approach based only on a proposal. In addition, the challenge afforded opportunities to communicate both agencies' interest in this topic for the purpose of encouraging private-sector development.

Participants: The challenge had 32 final entrants. Most were small teams, and four teams were from foreign countries despite clear messaging that only U.S. citizens or U.S.-based businesses were eligible to win the competition.

Timeline:
Phase 1 Open – 06/6/12
Phase 1 Close – 10/5/12
Phase 2 – 10/5/12 – 6/4/13

Solicitation and Outreach Methods and Results: Social media, promotions at conferences, and outreach to developer community were used. HHS's partner Health 2.0 and the EPA contractor for this challenge, InnoCentive, coordinated these outreach efforts. In addition, EPA and NIEHS both engaged the public with press releases, blog posts, and announcements, including the launch announcement at the 2012 HDI event in Washington, DC. The challenge was also published on the Popular Science Innovation Pavilion run by InnoCentive. The combination of all these efforts led to significant interest in the challenge – the primary registration and submission site, run by InnoCentive, saw the creation of over 500 project rooms, a proxy for the number of people interested enough to register to enter the challenge. The largest source (40%) of page views of the InnoCentive page came from the Popular Science Pavilion. Usage of the Pavilion worked well for the challenge; the science- and academic-heavy community it reaches matched up well with the very technical requirements of the challenge. The restriction of America COMPETES to U.S. citizens and businesses, however, mitigated the usefulness of the Pavilion, as the Pavilion reaches an international audience rather than focusing on a domestic audience.

Incentives: Finalists will be invited to an event providing feedback, presentations from subject matter experts, and networking. $60,000 for the Phase 1 cash prize purse came from EPA funds. $75,000 for the Phase 2 cash prize purse was drawn from ONC's Investing in Innovation (i2) contract with Capital Consulting Corporation. The remaining $25,000 for the Phase 2 cash prize purse came from NIEHS.

Evaluation:
The following Phase 1 criteria used to review the submissions:
- Strength of evidence regarding the linkage between air pollutant and physiological effect
- Viability of proposed sensor technologies to detect and quantify pollutants and their effects and to provide physiologically relevant health and air quality data
- Viability of the proposed project plan for producing a prototype
- Viability of the proposed instrument design as a wearable/portable device
- Potential significance of technology and eventual benefit to target population(s)
- Viability of the proposed proof-of-concept study (low complexity is preferred)
- Appropriate use of community input in designing proof-of-concept study

The following Phase 2 criteria used to review the finalist submissions:
- Sensors: Successful technical collection of both health and environmental data
- Data reporting: Successful formatting and transmission of data
- Data processing and evaluation
- Community involvement and interaction

Partnerships: ONC partnered with EPA and NIEHS to manage the challenge; EPA contracted with InnoCentive to provide challenge management services.

Resources: In addition to the cash prize purse, $550 in ONC travel funds will be used for transport to the finalist event held in Research Triangle Park, NC. One employee managed the challenge as a part of his overall challenge portfolio. NIEHS and EPA staff also participated in challenge management.

Results: Phase 1 was still open as of the close of FY 2012. Full competition results will be reported in the FY 2013 report to Congress. While the challenge is not yet complete, what has transpired so far has been successful – it has stimulated interest in the topic from a wide range of individuals and institutions including large companies, universities, athletics suppliers, and lone innovators. It demonstrates that the challenge mechanism is a viable platform for agency collaboration around a topic of mutual interest. The creation of the actual prototypes based on the finalists' proposals will be a key component in evaluating the success of the challenge and what lessons can be learned in future ones that involve physical work (as opposed to software and coding).

4. Department of Health and Human Services

4.1. SMART-Indivo Challenge

Overview: This challenge called on developers to build an Indivo application that provides value to patients using data delivered through the SMART API and its Indivo-specific extensions. Indivo is a free, open source, personally-controlled health record platform.[40] SMART (Substitutable Medical Apps, Reusable Technologies)[41] is one of four Strategic Health IT Advanced Research Projects (SHARP) funded by ONC. SMART facilitates innovation in health care by providing common APIs and standards for electronic medical records and personally controlled health records, enabling them to act as iPhone-like platforms; users can download or delete substitutable apps. Using the SMART API and standards, augmented by functionality like sharing, developers can create powerful patient-facing applications.

Website:
http://www.health2con.com/devchallenge/smart-indivo-app-challenge/

Problem Statement: The healthcare system is adapting to the effects of an aging population, growing expenditures, and a diminishing primary care workforce and needs the support of a flexible information infrastructure that facilitates innovation in wellness, health care, and public health. The challenge asked developers to create an Indivo app that could access patient demographics, medications, laboratory tests, and diagnoses using Web standards. Developers could, for example, build a medication manager, a health risk detector, a patient-friendly laboratory visualization tool, or an app that integrates external data sources (such as those found at http://www.healthdata.gov/) with patient records in real time.

Goal: This program was designed to test the challenge mechanism as a way to support an existing grant program.

Why a Prize as Preferred Method: The challenge mechanism was viewed as a way to generate proof-of-concept apps for the developer framework produced by an ONC grant. This would be a novel way to generate interest and awareness of the project and

---

[40] http://indivohealth.org/
[41] http://www.smartplatforms.org/

provide feedback on how developers unaffiliated with SMART viewed the framework. While the relatively small prize award may have put a ceiling on the amount of interest that would be generated, it also minimized the financial risk of an unsuccessful challenge.

Participants: The challenge had five entrants: one a single individual, others were small teams linked through their workplaces or small companies.

Timeline:
Open - 7/9/2012
Solicitation Close - 9/28/2012
Winners Announced - 11/30/2012

Solicitation and Outreach Methods and Results: Communications and outreach methods used include: social media (Twitter, Facebook, LinkedIn); outreach to the Health 2.0 Developer Community; a webinar discussing the challenge, framing issues, and Q&A; and conference promotion by Health 2.0. In addition, the SMART team at Harvard Medical School assisted by adding a challenge page to the project website.

Incentives:
- First Place: $10,000 & publicity from Health 2.0/ONC
- Second Place: $2,000
- Third Place: $1,000

Evaluation: A four-member review panel of individuals from the SMART team reviewed and scored each of the submissions using a web form that listed the evaluation criteria and their weights. Each criterion for each submission was rated from one (lowest) to five (highest), and a composite score was calculated; space for qualitative feedback was also included. Live demos of the top scorers were held via webinar to give the challenge managers the opportunity to ask additional questions of the potential winners that provided insight into the submissions, the developers, and their feedback on the challenge. The criteria used to review the submissions were:
- Usefulness to patients
- Importance to clinical medicine or public health
- Interface and presentation
- Use of the Indivo and SMART APIs
- Creative use of data from the sandbox and (optionally) from open health data sources

Partnerships: None

Resources: All funds were drawn from ONC's Investing in Innovation (i2) contract with Capital Consulting Corporation. No agency funding outside of the contract was used. One employee managed the challenge as a part of his overall challenge portfolio.

Results: Final winners were not announced by the end of FY 2012, and final competition results will be included in the FY 2013 prizes report to Congress.

4.2. EHR Accessibility Module Challenge

Overview: ONC challenged multidisciplinary teams to create and test a module or application that makes it easy for disabled consumers to access and interact with the health data stored in their Electronic Health Records (EHRs). According to 2000 estimates from the U.S. Bureau of Census, people with disabilities constitute 18.7 % of the non-institutionalized population. Among adults, individuals with disabilities are twelve times as likely to report having fair or poor health compared to those without a disability (47% vs. 4%). This population faces considerable difficulties with accessing and receiving care and the lack of coordinated care for this population is particularly costly. Health expenditures for people with disabilities are estimated at $400 billion, more than a quarter of all heath expenditures. Health information technology (HIT) and EHRs hold great promise in improving the health outcomes and coordination of care for people with disabilities. However, the accessibility and usability of HIT is a matter of concern to people of diverse disabilities, including those who have vision, hearing, intellectual, manual dexterity, mental health, developmental, and other types of disabilities. The disabled population cannot afford to miss out on the benefits that can be derived from having access to the health information stored in EHRs just because existing tools are not compliant with their needs. Building an accessible system from the ground up can be more cost effective than retrofitting current ones to suit this large group and can prevent future interoperability issues. In addition, innovation in this area can also help older individuals with changing abilities due to aging, and can help inspire usability improvements for all consumers on a more general basis.

Website:
http://www.health2con.com/devchallenge/ehr-accessibility-module/

Problem Statement: The challenge was for multidisciplinary teams to create and test a module or application that makes it easy for disabled consumers to access and interact with the health data stored in their EHRs. The application was to:
- Be easy for individuals with disabilities to interact with their health data
- Be simple to install and learn to use
- Identify and link to relevant local or online communities and organizations
- Be able to download data from one or more EHR systems – it did not need to be fully integrated across all systems

Goal: Improve service delivery

<u>Why a Prize as Preferred Method</u>: The prize mechanism was chosen because the advantages that come from open innovation were deemed more appropriate for the project than sole-source acquisition. These advantages include focusing the developer community on a high priority topic, leveraging developers' creativity and knowledge of what makes successful apps rather than choosing a team or approach at the outset of the project and then having to stick with it, and using the public nature of the challenge mechanism to draw attention to the topic through live and social media announcements. Since one of the goals of the project was simply to create more potential solutions for stakeholders, a contract or grant that would have resulted in only one solution being created would not have been appropriate.

<u>Participants</u>: The challenge had five entrants, all of which were small teams linked through their workplaces or were small companies.

<u>Timeline</u>:
Submission Open -- 1/30/2012
Submission Close -- 7/23/2012
Winners Announced -- 8/13/2012

<u>Solicitation and Outreach Methods and Results</u>: Communications and outreach methods used include social media (Twitter, Facebook, LinkedIn); outreach to the Health 2.0 Developer Community; a webinar discussing the challenge, framing issues, and Q&A; and conference promotion by Health 2.0. The challenge was run in collaboration with HHS' Office on Disability, which also promoted the challenge in its own communications. Subject matter experts from NIST and Access Board also assisted with outreach.

<u>Incentives</u>: Exhibition opportunity at relevant conference or event and $70,000 total cash prizes; all funds were drawn from ONC's Investing in Innovation (i2) contract with Capital Consulting Corporation.

<u>Evaluation</u>: A four-member review panel composed of individuals representing NIST, Access Board, HHS' Office on Disability, and CMS reviewed and scored each of the submissions against the weighted evaluation criteria. Live demos of the top scorers were held via webinar to give the challenge managers the opportunity to ask additional questions of the potential winners that provided insight into the submissions, the developers, and their feedback on the challenge.

The criteria used to review the submissions were:
- Design and usability for the disabled user
- Creative and innovative use of technologies
- Compliance with disability and accessibility standards including 508 and W3C
- Integration of module with HIT and EHR systems
- Potential for impact and ability to drive adoption and engagement

Partnerships: Formal partnerships were not established for this challenge, but the organizations of the subject matter experts (NIST, Access Board, and HHS Office on Disability) assisted in communications and outreach.

Resources: No agency funding outside of the contract was used. One employee managed the challenge as a part of his overall challenge portfolio.

Results: This challenge sought to advance the agency mission by improving access to personal health data for people with disabilities. While the winner met expectations, the submissions for this challenge were fewer than other similar i2 challenges and of lower quality – several submissions simply used the built-in accessibility features of operating systems and made only small tweaks to their already-existing products. This may have been due to low interest in the developer community or the fact that the i2 program was running multiple challenges concurrently, giving developers several to choose to participate in, thereby capping the number of developers that would submit for each.

4.3. Discharge Follow-Up Appointment Challenge

Overview: In order to support broader adoption and uptake of promising IT-enabled interventions that address care transitions, ONC challenged software developers to create an easy-to-use web-based tool to make post-discharge follow-up appointment scheduling an effective process for care providers, patients, and caregivers. Nearly one in five patients from a hospital will be readmitted within 30 days. A large proportion of readmissions can be prevented by improving communications and coordinating care before and after discharge from the hospital. Research has shown that scheduling follow-up appointments and post-discharge testing before a patient is discharged is one of the critical elements of a safe and effective transition. Most patients across the country continue to leave the hospital without confirmed appointments and many providers remain frustrated by a highly manual and unreliable system. Communities struggling with the process of scheduling and securing these appointments have articulated challenges faced by the following stakeholders:

- *Patients and caregivers*: Lack of involvement in transition process leading to lack of understanding of appointment necessity, scheduling conflicts, transportation difficulties, and high risk of cancelation or no-shows.
- *Discharging hospital provider*: Inability to see appointment availability to assist patient and caregiver with scheduling (resulting in the need for multiple phone calls), resistance from downstream providers while trying to secure appointment for harder to place/high risk patients, lack of feedback if a no-show or cancellation occurs, and burden of multiple post-discharge needs.
- *Downstream provider*: High no-show rates or cancelations, lack of predictability of appointment requests from discharging hospital provider, and lack of information regarding high-risk or harder to place patients.

A growing number of innovative consumer-facing tools are becoming available for patients and care givers to schedule appointments and rate providers. However, these tools have not yet reached high levels of adoption within communities, and to date have not targeted the appointment scheduling needs of patients, caregivers, and providers at the point of discharge from a hospital.

Website:
http://www.health2con.com/devchallenge/discharge-follow-up-appointment-challenge/

Problem Statement: In order to support broader adoption and uptake of promising IT-enabled interventions that address care transitions, ONC challenged software developers to create an easy-to-use web-based tool to make post-discharge follow-up appointment scheduling a more effective and shared process for care providers, patients and caregivers. In addition, developers needed to articulate a plan for broader adoption at the community level. The ideal application would include the following components:
- Easy to navigate user interface
- Easy to navigate process for downstream accepting providers
- Information for patient and caregiver convenience and preference
- Critical background information for downstream provider
- Messaging capabilities to minimize no-shows and cancellations
- EHR interface capabilities where applicable

To anticipate the needs of a test bed organization or community, successful applicants also needed to submit a brief pilot implementation proposal (250-500 words) that addresses factors including timeline, description of pilot environment needs, and additional resource needs.

Goal: Improve service delivery

Why a Prize as Preferred Method: The prize mechanism was chosen because the advantages that come from open innovation were deemed more appropriate for the project than sole-source acquisition, as described above. In this case, one of the goals of the challenge was simply to create a greater number of potential solutions from which stakeholders could choose; a contract or grant would have resulted in only one.

Participants: The challenge had 13 entrants. Entrants were for the most part small teams (three to five people) linked through school or workplace, or small companies.

Timeline:
Solicitation Open – 1/26/2012
Solicitation Close – 4/30/2012
Winners Announced – 5/23/2012

<u>Solicitation and Outreach Methods and Results</u>: Communications and outreach methods used include social media (Twitter, Facebook, LinkedIn); outreach to the Health 2.0 Developer Community; a webinar discussing the challenge, framing issues, and Q&A; and conference promotion by Health 2.0. The challenge was also communicated directly to care transitions stakeholders at transitions-specific meetings. Considering the challenge's technical complexity and the prizes offered, the number of submissions received was within the range of expectations. Challenge organizers suspect that one reason provider-oriented challenges tend to receive fewer submissions than consumer-targeted ones is that the former are less likely to garner the mainstream attention.

<u>Incentives</u>: Partnership consideration with a pilot test bed community candidate; three-day site visit to the pilot community; and $5,000 total cash prizes. All funds were drawn from ONC's Investing in Innovation (i2) contract with Capital Consulting Corporation.

<u>Evaluation</u>: A six-member review panel composed of individuals representing care transitions organizations and ONC reviewed and scored each of the submissions using a web form that listed the evaluation criteria and their weights. Live demos of the top scorers were held via webinar to give the challenge managers the opportunity to ask additional questions of the potential winners that provided insight into the submissions, the developers, and their feedback on the challenge.

The criteria used to review the submissions were:
- Effectively integrate inpatient data and provide structured support for self-care
- Integrate design and usability concepts to drive patient and provider adoption and engagement
- Demonstrate creative and innovative uses of mobile technologies
- Demonstrate potential to improve health status for individuals and the community
- Leverage NwHIN standards including transport, content, and vocabularies
- Demonstrate ability to implement the intervention in a pilot setting, and ultimately to scale in a community.

<u>Partnerships</u>: ONC was assisted by the Partnership for Patients (a CMS-led initiative) in communications activities.

<u>Resources</u>: No agency funding outside of the contract was used. One employee managed the challenge as a part of his overall challenge portfolio.

<u>Results</u>: This challenge advanced the agency's mission by creating numerous new tools[42] for providers to use to reduce patient readmissions through effective appointment scheduling. Reduction in readmissions due to usage of these tools will result in improved patient health and lowering of health care costs. The top submissions all

---

[42] http://www.health2con.com/devchallenge/discharge-follow-up-appointment-challenge/

included easy-to-use, synchronized scheduling tools for providers, consumers, and caretakers while also providing assorted other functionalities that appeal to different types of stakeholders, including integration with multi-purpose patient portals, appointment transportation coordination, and automated reminders. The First Place winning application, MyHealthDIRECT, is a web-based solution that effectively matches the demand for health care appointments with a supply of actual appointment slots.

4.4. Reporting Patient Safety Events

Overview: Hospitals and other health care organizations have multiple adverse event reporting relationships with Patient Safety Organizations (PSO), state agencies, and the FDA. Hospitals struggle to increase internal incident reporting, especially by busy care providers, and to create effective systems for the quality and risk management staff to complete root cause analyses and follow-up which are required by both CMS and the Joint Commission. Quality and risk management staff suffer from reporting fatigue in a paper-based reporting system, which affects reporting frequency and quality – much effort is spent on convincing physicians and nurses to report incidents, complete investigations, fill out the appropriate forms, and fax them to the appropriate agencies.

These reporting issues could be partially alleviated through the deployment of an effective software reporting solution. Solutions would need to make it easier for any qualified individual to file a report electronically and must allow the hospital quality and risk management staff to add information from follow-up investigation, submit reports as appropriate to PSOs, the state, or the FDA, and track follow-up activities.

Website:
http://www.health2con.com/devchallenge/reporting-patient-safety-events-challenge/

Problem Statement: The challenge asked multi-disciplinary teams to develop an application that facilitates the reporting of patient safety events, whether implemented in hospital or ambulatory settings.

To qualify to win, applications needed to:
- Increase the ease of reporting patient safety events to the provider or parent organization.
- Enable providers to import relevant EHR, personal health record, and other electronic information, including screen shots, to the patient safety report and, in turn, submit an Agency for Healthcare Research and Quality (AHRQ) Common Formats-compliant report to one or more PSOs.
- Capture useful demographic and other relevant information from each patient including age, gender, race, and relevant diagnoses.
- Capture information about the type of organization submitting the report using AHRQ's PSO Information format.

- Reduce burden of reporting by enabling the provider or parent organization to have the option of submitting information in the patient safety report to non-PSO public health or health oversight organizations, including state or federal programs or accrediting or certifying bodies.
- Be platform-agnostic; and
- Leverage and extend NwHIN standards and services including, but not limited to, transport (Direct, web services), content (Transitions of Care, CCD/CCR), and standardized vocabularies.

Goal: Improve service delivery

Why a Prize as Preferred Method: The prize mechanism was chosen because the advantages that come from open innovation were deemed more appropriate for the project than sole-source acquisition, as described above. Like i2 challenges, it was important to seed the space with a number of different solutions and give providers a handful of options, with varying functionalities, from which to choose.

Participants: The challenge had 13 entrants. Entrants were for the most part small teams (three to five people) linked through school or workplace, or small companies.

Timeline:
Solicitation Open – 4/12/2012
Solicitation Close – 8/31/2012
Winners Announced – 11/14/2012

Solicitation and Outreach Methods and Results: Communications and outreach methods used include social media (Twitter, Facebook, LinkedIn); outreach to the Health 2.0 Developer Community; a webinar discussing the challenge, framing issues, and Q&A; and conference promotion by Health 2.0. The challenge was also communicated directly to patient safety stakeholders at safety-specific meetings. Considering the challenge's technical complexity and the incentives offered, the number of submissions received was within the range of expectations.

Incentives: Exhibition opportunity at relevant conference or event and $70,000 total cash prizes; all funds were drawn from ONC's Investing in Innovation (i2) contract with Capital Consulting Corporation.

Evaluation: A five-member review panel representing AHRQ, ONC, and FDA reviewed and scored each of the submissions against weighted evaluation criteria. Live demos of the top scorers were held via webinar to give the challenge managers the opportunity to ask additional questions of the potential winners that provided insight into the submissions, the developers, and their feedback on the challenge. Including members of the review panel on the live demos helped facilitate post-challenge activities and outreach about the challenge and winners.

Partnerships: Following the conclusion of the challenge, AHRQ provided assistance in communicating the winners and their solutions to appropriate stakeholders and potential customers.

Resources: No agency funding outside of the contract was used. One employee managed the challenge as a part of his overall challenge portfolio.

Results: The challenge helped the agency mission by creating new tools that advance the ability of providers, particularly busy hospitals, to report safety events. Like several other provider-oriented i2 challenges, these tools provide solutions where either there weren't any before or the products available were not sufficient to enact meaningful change. Adoption of these tools will also help spread the use of AHRQ's Common Formats, promoting a standard that will make exchange of safety reports a smoother and easier process in the future.

4.5. popHealth Tool Development Challenge

Overview: Under the Health Information Technology for Economic and Clinical Health (HITECH) Act, eligible health care professionals and hospitals can qualify for Medicare and Medicaid incentive payments when they adopt certified EHR technology and use it to achieve specified objectives. These "Meaningful Use" objectives include measureable benchmarks providers must meet to qualify for the incentive payments. popHealth is an open source software service developed under the guidance of the Office of the National Coordinator for Health Information Technology (ONC) that automates the reporting of the Stage 1 Meaningful Use clinical quality measures. popHealth integrates with a healthcare provider's electronic health record (EHR) system using continuity of care records. It streamlines the automated generation of summary quality measure reports on the provider's patient population. ONC challenged software developers to create applications that leveraged the popHealth open source framework, existing functionality, standards, and sample datasets to improve patient care and provide greater insight into patient populations.

Website:
http://www.health2challenge.org/pophealth-tool-development-challenge/

Problem Statement: ONC challenged software developers to create applications that leveraged the popHealth open source framework, existing functionality, standards, and sample datasets to improve patient care and provide insight into patient populations.

Applications were to accomplish at least one of the following:
* Help providers improve patient safety
* Help providers use quality measure calculations to better engage with patients
* Help providers address disparities in the care they provide to their patient populations

- Help providers engage patients and families
- Aggregate data from across multiple sites to allow public health entities to develop a more clearly defined picture of community health status and risk factors
- Visualize information in the popHealth system related to meaningful use measures
- Target patients with high disease burden in need of early intervention

Goal: Improve service delivery.

Why a Prize as Preferred Method: The prize mechanism was chosen because the advantages that come from open innovation were deemed more appropriate for the project than sole-source acquisition, as described above. This aspect was particularly relevant here since one of the goals of the challenge was to increase awareness of the popHealth tool in general and increase its adoption and usage by providers.

Participants: The challenge had 11 entrants. Entrants were for the most part small teams (three to five people) linked through school or workplace, or small companies.

Timeline:
Solicitation Open – 10/3/2011
Solicitation Close – 1/21/2012
Winners Announced – 2/20/2012

Solicitation and Outreach Methods and Results: Communications and outreach methods used include social media (Twitter, Facebook, LinkedIn); outreach to the Health 2.0 Developer Community; a webinar discussing the challenge, framing issues, and Q&A; and conference promotion by Health 2.0. The MITRE Corp. also helped spread the word to developer networks.

Incentives: Exhibition opportunity at relevant conference or event and $100,000 total cash prizes; all funds were drawn from ONC's Investing in Innovation (i2) contract with Capital Consulting Corporation.

Evaluation: A five-member review panel including representatives from ONC reviewed and scored each of the submissions against weighted criteria. Live demos of the top scorers were held via webinar to give the challenge managers the opportunity to ask additional questions of the potential winners that provided insight into the submissions, the developers, and their feedback on the challenge.

The criteria used to review the submissions were:
- Ability to integrate with popHealth system and build upon existing functionality
- Impact on stakeholders
- Usability and design from the standpoint of all stakeholders
- Creativity and innovation

Partnerships: ONC's contractor MITRE Corp. developed the original popHealth framework and tool, so it was engaged to help market the challenge and to answer questions from potential solvers. Unsurprisingly, it was very helpful to have the experts on popHealth available to handle specific technical questions.

Resources: No agency funding outside of the contract was used. One employee and one detailee managed the challenge as a part of their overall challenge portfolio.

Results: This challenge advanced the agency mission by helping to make it easier for providers to report Meaningful Use clinical quality measures. Solutions were of high quality, due in part to the clean graphics of and ease of developing for the popHealth framework. They provided new functionalities for the tool which otherwise would have been done by MITRE, at higher contractor costs. However, long-term success for this challenge is highly dependent on adoption of the basic popHealth tool.

4.6. One in a Million Hearts Challenge

Overview: Cardiovascular disease is the leading cause of death in America. The goal of the Million Hearts initiative is to prevent one million heart attacks and strokes over five years by reducing the number of people who need treatment and improving the quality of treatment for those who do need it. To achieve this goal, a range of programs will be targeted toward improving care of the **ABCS**: "**A**" for aspirin therapy for people at high risk, "**B**" for blood pressure control, "**C**" for cholesterol management, and "**S**" for smoking cessation. This challenge is a multidisciplinary call to innovators and developers to create an application that activates and empowers patients to get healthy and improve their heart health using the ABCS.

Website:
http://www.health2challenge.org/one-in-a-million-hearts-challenge/

Problem Statement:
Submissions were required to:
- Provide information about the Million Hearts initiative
- Have patients enter relevant information about their health such as age, body mass index, blood pressure, cholesterol level, smoking status, pertinent medical history, aspirin, and cholesterol-lowering agent use
- Use the patient-reported data and ABCS framework to generate targeted recommendations to the patient such as providing education and resources to help reduce fat and salt intake, increase exercise, lose weight, stop smoking, or increase medication adherence (e.g., to improve control of high blood pressure); using GPS technology to recommend nearby walks or places to eat healthier; recommending to

the high-risk patient to see a primary care doctor if not on aspirin or cholesterol-lowering medication; or linking to online heart-health communities
- Be able to send patient information to electronic health records via Direct[43]

Goal: Solve a health problem(s)

Why a Prize as Preferred Method: The prize mechanism was chosen because the advantages that come from open innovation, as described above, were deemed more appropriate for the project than sole-source acquisition.

Participants: The challenge had 19 entrants. Entrants were for the most part small teams (three to five people) linked through school or workplace, or small companies.

Timeline:
Solicitation Opened: 10/3/2011
Solicitation Closed: 1/1/2012
Winners Announced: 3/25/2012

Solicitation and Outreach Methods and Results: Communications and outreach methods used include social media (Twitter, Facebook, LinkedIn); outreach to the Health 2.0 Developer Community; a webinar discussing the challenge, framing issues, and Q&A; and conference promotion (American College of Cardiology Conference).

Incentives: Exhibition opportunity at relevant conference or event and $75,000 total cash prizes. All funds were drawn from ONC's Investing in Innovation (i2) contract with Capital Consulting Corporation.

Evaluation: A seven-member review panel representing an assortment of heart health-related organizations, including American Heart Association, American College of Cardiology, and the National Heart, Lung, and Blood Institute, reviewed and scored each of the submissions against weighted evaluation criteria. Since the submission package was a demo video and descriptive slides rather than an actual, publically available app, after the top finishers were determined live demos were held via webinar to prove that the solutions were not vaporware. In addition to the confirmation aspect, the demos allowed the challenge managers to ask questions of the potential winners that provided insight into the submissions, the developers, and their feedback on the challenge.

The criteria used to review the submissions were:
- Patient engagement
- Quality and accessibility of information and resources
- Targeted and actionable information

---

[43] http://directproject.org

49

- Innovativeness and Usability
- Bonus points awarded for creating both English and Spanish versions

Partnerships: ONC partnered with the Million Hearts Initiative, an intra-HHS partnership, for their subject-matter expertise and communications and outreach channels.

Resources: No agency funding outside of the contract was used. One employee and one detailee managed the challenge as a part of their overall challenge portfolio.

Results: This challenge advanced the agency mission by empowering individuals to improve their health using health IT tools. The submissions demonstrated a range of approaches to this type of tool, including websites, mobile-optimized sites, mobile phone apps, augmentations and additions to personal health portals, and SMS/text messages.

4.7. What's in your Health Record Video Challenge

Overview: Video competition to inspire members of the public to develop short videos sharing a story about why having access to review what is in a patient's health record can improve that patient's quality of care or the care of a loved one. Patients have a legal right under HIPAA to request to see and get a copy of their health info from their health care providers. However, awareness about this right is low.

Website:
http://yourrecord.challenge.gov/

Problem Statement: This competition was one method of increasing awareness about patients' legal right to get access to their medical records from their health care providers in an electronic format, if available. Participants were asked to provide a specific example (personal story, experience, testimonial, or thoughtful idea) of the benefits of having access to view their health record and the ability to review what's in their health record. The video had to encourage viewers to visit www.HealthIT.gov and to ask their health care provider to see and get a copy of their medical record.

Goal: Public education

Why a Prize as Preferred Method: Challenge organizers wanted to crowd-source compelling personal stories from the public that could potentially motivate and inspire others to adopt health IT and eHealth tools to be more engaged with their health care provider and to take a more active role in their own health and health care. Organizers also wanted to increase awareness about the role that health IT can play in people's lives, and the challenge generated press and web traffic, which elevated awareness of their Consumer eHealth program and started a viral conversation about the value of health IT. Prize money helped to attract a diversity of people to participate in these competitions — from a range of different ethnicities, ages and geographies.

Participants: 31 eligible submissions; 1/3 of entrants were teams, the rest were individuals.

Timeline:
Solicitation Open – 7/9/2012
Solicitation Close – 8/23/2012
Winner Announced – 9/10/2012

Solicitation and Outreach Methods and Results: Newsletters and targeted emails to more than 300,000 registered users in the ChallengePost network. Targeted outreach via email and social media channels to influencers, hackathon organizers, and developer communities on Twitter, Facebook, LinkedIn, Google+, Google Groups, and Meetup. Weekly/bi-weekly targeted emails to the registrants and followers, providing reminders on important dates and tips on getting started. Leveraged all ONC communication channels, including ONC list-serv of 58K subscribers, blog, and social media channels.

Incentives: Prize purse was $7700 (5 awards: First Prize $3K, 2nd Prize $2K, 3rd Prize $1K, 2 honorable mention awards of $500); Money to oversee the competitions and allocate prize money was provided through a contract with RTI funded with FY12 funds.

Evaluation: A four-person panel evaluated submissions. Each submission was evaluated on a scale of 1-5 on each of the following criteria: 1) quality of story and 2) potential impact on motivating others to access their health record.

Partnerships: None

Resources: 20% of 1 FTE staffer to oversee the contract and assist with marketing and outreach support for each competition, including the recruitment of partners. Contract support provided by RTI, who sub-contracted to ChallengePost.

Results: Scripting, shooting, and editing two-minute promotional videos costs, on average, about $10,000. This competition received 31 eligible video submissions – potentially $310,000 worth of promotional material and over 40 times the $7,700 in prize money awarded. In addition, the attention received, both mainstream and within the participating communities, was valuable. The challenge received hundreds of social media mentions as well as mainstream media exposure. The winning videos combined were viewed over 1,909 times. The challenge website received over 25K page views, over 7K site visits, and over 947 followers. Over 750 votes were cast by the public for submissions to determine the Popular Choice winner.

4.8.   Managing Meds Video Challenge

Overview: The Managing Meds Video Challenge invited the public to create short, inspiring videos sharing how they have used technology to manage taking medications effectively or to support individuals to take their medications as directed. There are serious consequences for patients from not taking medications as prescribed.

Website:
http://managingmeds.challenge.gov/

Problem Statement: Consumers or patients could participate by creating a less than two minute video demonstrating how they can use technology for medication management.

Goal: Public education

Why a Prize as Preferred Method: Challenge organizers wanted to crowd-source compelling personal stories from the public that could potentially motivate and inspire others to adopt health IT and eHealth tools to be more engaged with their health care provider and to take a more active role in their own health and health care. Challenge organizers also wanted to increase awareness about the role that health IT can play in people's lives. The competitions generated press and a lot of web traffic, which elevated awareness of their Consumer eHealth, program and started a viral conversation about the value of health IT. The competition both about the videos that were generated and about getting the public talking about the role patients could play in their health by leveraging technology. Prize money helped to attract a diversity of people to participate in these competitions — from a range of different ethnicities, ages, and geographies.

Participants: Members of the public and health care professionals were the targets of this competition. Registration was open for 10-weeks. Entrants: 21 eligible submissions. Only about 1/4 of entrants were teams, the rest were individuals.

Timeline:
Solicitation Opened – 8/10/2012
Solicitation Closed – 10/19/2012
Winners Announced – 11/13/2012

Solicitation and Outreach Methods and Results: ONC leveraged its communication channels, including Buzz Blog; an email mailing list; and social media, such as targeted outreach to influencers, hackathon organizers, and developer communities on Twitter, Facebook, LinkedIn, Google+, Google Groups, and Meetup. The competition's partner, Script Your Future, conducted outreach to member organizations and to pharmacy schools to support the competition. Newsletters and targeted emails were sent to more than 300,000 registered users in the ChallengePost network. Weekly/bi-weekly targeted emails were sent to the registrants and followers, providing reminders on important dates and tips on getting started. One lesson learned is to try to time submission period to correspond with dates in which potential participants will be the most engaged (ex. when pharmacy schools are in session).

Incentives: $7,500 total: $3K for first place, $2K for second place; $1K for third place; $500 for two Honorable Mentions; and $500 for a Popular Choice award.

Evaluation: A three-person panel evaluated submissions. Each submission was evaluated on a scale of 1-5 on each of the following criteria: 1) Quality of the idea; 2) Implementation of the idea, and 3) Potential impact on health IT adoption.

Partnerships: Script Your Future

Resources: 20% of 1 FTE federal person to oversee the contract and assist with marketing and outreach support for each competition, including the recruitment of partners. Contract support provided by RTI, who sub-contracted to ChallengePost.

Results: The window for submissions was still open at the end of FY 2012, so competition results will be reported in the FY 2013 prizes report to Congress.

4.9. Healthy People 2020 Leading Health Indicators App Challenge

Overview: The HHS Office of Disease Prevention and Health Promotion (ODPHP) and ONC challenged teams of developers and health professionals to co-design an application that will be used to help solve one or more of their Nation's high-priority health problems as part of HHS's Healthy People 2020 initiative.[44]

Website:
http://www.health2con.com/devchallenge/healthy-people-2020-leading-health-indicators-app-challenge/

Problem Statement: The challenge aimed to address one or more of the 12 leading health indicator (LHI) topics by encouraging health professionals to work with developers in designing an application that could be used to address the indicators at the community level. To enter the competition, participants had to create an application that makes health indicators customizable and easy to use.

Goal: Solve a health problem(s)

---

[44] http://www.healthypeople.gov

Why a Prize as Preferred Method: A prize competition was developed in order to encourage ideas about how leading health indicators can be addressed in innovative ways and to inspire quick responses from software application developers.

Participants: The challenge aimed to mobilize developers while also engaging health professionals and stakeholders through a collaborative, co-designing process. Subject matter experts with an idea for an app were encouraged to reach out to developers and designers to turn their ideas into a reality. There were 16 final submissions. Most entries represented a company, and the winning teams ranged from 2-6 team members.

Timeline:
Solicitation Open – 10/31/2011
Solicitation Close – 03/09/2012
Winners Announced – 3/30/2012

Solicitation and Outreach Methods and Results: ODPHP conducted outreach via Healthy People 2020 e-blasts, Twitter, and LinkedIn. ODPHP and ONC worked with Health 2.0 to reach out to the developer community via Health 2.0's outreach channels. Challenge organizers also reached out to academia and engaging students or young developers. HHS hosted a one-hour Webinar for interested participants to learn more about challenge requirements and criteria.

Incentives: An opportunity to provide an app demo at the 2012 National Health Promotion Summit. $15,000 total cash prizes were allocated through a sub-contract.

Evaluation: The prize competition utilized the following judging criteria: easy access; platform neutrality; user appeal; innovation of design; broad applicability; integration of health data; evidence of co-design and collaboration, and accessibility.

Partnerships: ODPHP and ONC had a subcontract with Health 2.0 to administer the challenge.

Resources: ONC provided $15K to Health 2.0 to pay for administering and marketing the challenge to developers and stakeholders. ODPHP provided $15K honorariums that allowed the winners to come to the National Health Promotion Summit in April 2012 to demo their app among stakeholders.

Results: The prize competition advanced the main purpose of the leading health indicators, which is to communicate the nation's high-priority health issues, and actions that can be taken to address them. The challenge provided visibility around this set of indicators, and encouraged Healthy People stakeholders to start problem-solving by thinking about creative solutions to addressing important health issues. The final three winners were Community Commons, PhenotypeIT, and Trilogy[45]. The First Place Community Commons application offers an interactive mapping, networking, and learning utility to leaders from community to national levels. The application seeks to help create informed, healthy, equitable, and sustainable communities. Key features include an interactive initiatives map and an array of starter maps tools that to track place-based around the country.

4.10. Beat Down Blood Pressure Video Challenge

Overview: ONC hosted this video competition to encourage members of the public to share their personal stories about how they are using health IT to manage high blood pressure and to crowd-source stories about which tools that prevent or manage high blood pressure.

Website:
http://bloodpressure.challenge.gov/

Problem Statement: Participants were asked to make a video describing how they use health IT or consumer e-health tools to prevent or manage high blood pressure. Individuals and teams who comply with rules were eligible to participate. There were several categories and associated prize money. There were three categories for consumers to enter using health IT for: (1) monitoring; (2) taking meds; and (3) preventing high blood pressure. Plus, there were two categories with prizes for health care providers to enter: (1) provider monitoring; and (2) provider medication management.

Goal: Public education

Why a Prize as Preferred Method: Challenge organizers wanted to crowd-source compelling personal stories from the public that could potentially motivate and inspire others to adopt health IT and eHealth tools to be more engaged with their health care provider and to take a more active role in their own health and health care. Challenge organizers also wanted to increase awareness about health IT.

Participants: The competition was aimed at all Americans, although challenge organizers suspected there would be greater interest from individuals who have a personal connection to high blood pressure — either themselves or a family history of dealing with the disease. Challenge organizers received 14 eligible submissions — only one team entered, the rest were individuals. Prize money helped to attract a diversity of people to participate from a range of different ethnicities, ages, and geographies.

---

[45] http://www.health2con.com/devchallenge/healthy-people-2020-leading-health-indicators-app-challenge/

Timeline:
Solicitation Open – 3/28/2012
Solicitation Close – 5/16/2012
Winners Announced – 6/15/2012

Solicitation and Outreach Methods and Results: Newsletters and targeted emails to more than 300,000 registered users in the ChallengePost network. Targeted outreach via email and social media channels to influencers, hackathon organizers, and developer communities on Twitter, Facebook, LinkedIn, Google+, Google Groups, and Meetup. Weekly/bi-weekly targeted emails to the registrants and followers, providing reminders on important dates and tips on getting started.

Incentives: *$4,500 available.* Money to oversee the competitions and allocate prize money was provided through a contract with RTI funded with FY12 funds.

Evaluation: Submissions were evaluated by a four-person panel. Each submission was evaluated against criteria including quality of idea; implementation of idea, and potential impact on health IT adoption.

Partnerships: American Heart Association and Million Hearts

Resources: 20% of 1 FTE federal person to oversee the contract and assist with marketing and outreach support for each competition, including the recruitment of partners. Contract support provided by RTI, who sub-contracted to ChallengePost.

Results: Scripting, shooting, and editing a two-minute promotional video costs, on average, about $10,000. The ONC Blood Pressure Video Challenge received 14 eligible video submissions – potentially $140,000 worth of promotional material and 31 times the $4,500 in prize money awarded. The attention received, both mainstream and within the participating communities, elevated awareness of the Consumer eHealth program and started a viral conversation about the value of health IT. The challenge received hundreds of social media mentions as well as mainstream media exposure. There were nearly 19,000 page views, over 7,000 site visits, nearly 1,500 votes cast for submissions to determine the Popular Choice Award winner, 593 followers, 81 "Accepted the Challenge" to receive submitter updates, 14 eligible video submissions, and 5 winners. This impact helps advance ONC's goal of increasing consumer awareness about the value of health IT and driving greater adoption and use of eHealth. The winning videos combined were viewed over 1,735 times.

4.11.   Healthy New Year Challenge

Overview: This challenge was a call for ordinary Americans to create short videos that captured their New Year's resolution and how they plan to leverage technology to achieve their goal. The purpose of the video competition is to crowd-source personal stories from the public to motivate and inspire others to adopt and use health IT.

Website:
http://healthynewyear.challenge.gov

Problem Statement: Develop a short video focused on a health-related New Year's Resolution and describe how health IT will be used to help achieve that goal. In addition, the video had to point to HealthIT.gov for more information.

Goal: Public education

Why a Prize as Preferred Method: The prize added an incentive for ordinary Americans to share their personal story/testimonial about how they were leveraging health IT to improve their health and health care. Challenge organizers wanted to crowd source authentic stories from the public and engage the public in voting and sharing these videos to help generate greater awareness of the value of health IT and the role that eHealth can play in helping people take more control of their health.

Participants: Challenge organizers goal was to mobilize a diversity of participants from a variety of demographics and ethnicities. Anyone over the age of 18 years old was eligible to participate. They received 47 eligible submissions from a diversity of demographics and ethnicities.

Timeline:
Solicitation Open – 1/9/2012
Solicitation Closed – 2/16/2012
Winners Announced – 3/22/2012

Solicitation and Outreach Methods and Results: Issued an official HHS Press release to announce this competition as the first in a series of health IT video competitions that would occur throughout 2012. Challenge organizers leveraged ONC communication channels, including the Health IT Buzz Blog, the ONC List Serve (around 58K subscribers), and social media outreach through Twitter to mobilize participation. In addition, ChallengePost also conducted its own outreach to followers of its other competitions. There were over 100,000 page views throughout the competition period; more than 25,000 site visits; greater than 10,000 votes cast for submissions to determine the Popular Choice Award winner; 1,042 followers of the competition; 111 "Accepted the Challenge" to receive submitter updates; 47 eligible video submissions; and 7 winners.

Incentives: $2000 - 1st, $1000 - 2nd, $500-3rd, $250 - Honorable Mention (2), $750 - Popular Choice; FY12 funds supported a contract to administer these challenges.

Evaluation: Judges evaluated each submission based on the quality of the idea, the implementation of the idea, and the potential impact on health IT adoption.

Partnerships: None

Resources: 1 FTE dedicated about 20% of her time to oversee the video competition series throughout 2012. A contract was awarded to RTI for administering the competitions, which included prize money. RTI sub-contracted to ChallengePost.

Results: This video competition helped increase awareness about how consumers can leverage health IT to accelerate and support greater engagement in their health and health care. This competition generated over 100K views and impressions to the site as well as a number of press related articles in the trade publications. The 2nd place winning video has been used on multiple occasions by senior level ONC staff in presentations and has received rave reviews. Scripting, shooting, and editing two-minute promotional videos costs, on average, about $10,000. The ONC Health New Year Video Challenge received 47 eligible video submissions – potentially $470,000 worth of promotional material and 94 times the $5,000 in prize money awarded. The winning videos combined were viewed over 4,438 times.

4.12. Design by Biomedical Undergraduate Teams (DEBUT) Challenge

Overview: The National Institute of Biomedical Imaging and Bioengineering (NIBIB) and the National Institutes of Health (NIH) challenged teams of undergraduate students to design and build innovative solutions to unmet health and clinical problems. Entries were solicited in three challenge categories, diagnostics; therapeutics; and technology, to aid underserved populations and individuals with disabilities. The winning team in each category received a $10,000 prize, and was honored at an award ceremony during the 2012 Annual Meeting of the Biomedical Engineering Society in Atlanta, GA. In each category, challenge organizers also identified two honorable mentions with no accompanying monetary prize. The goals of the challenge were to: (1) provide undergraduate students valuable experiences such as working in teams, identifying unmet clinical needs, and designing, building and debugging solutions for such open-ended problems; (2) generate novel tools to improve healthcare, consistent with NIBIB's purpose to support research, training, dissemination of health information, and other programs with respect to biomedical imaging and engineering; and (3) highlight and acknowledge accomplishments of undergraduate students. DEBUT is the only competition focused on biomedical design and open only to undergraduate students.

Website:
debut.challenge.gov

Problem Statement: The problem addressed by the challenge was the design of innovative solutions to unmet health and clinical problems in three categories:

diagnostic devices and methods; therapeutic devices and methods; and technology to aid underserved populations and individuals with disabilities. Teams composed of at least 3 undergraduate students in Biomedical Engineering and related fields were eligible to compete with original designs developed solely by them. The entries were judged on the significance of the problem addressed, impact on potential users, innovativeness of design, and the evidence of a working prototype.

Goal: Improved service delivery; public education; and engagement of teams of undergraduate students in open-ended biomedical design projects.

Why a Prize as Preferred Method: The prize mechanism was used as a complement to other mechanisms already used by their agency, to directly engage and excite students.

Participants: The targeted participants were undergraduate students in Biomedical Engineering and related fields. Challenge organizers received entries from 61 student teams made up of a total of 284 students from 39 different universities.

Timeline:
Solicitation Open – 1/3/2012
Solicitation Close – 6/2/2012
Winners Announced – 7/31/2012
Award Ceremony – 10/26/2012

Solicitation and Outreach Methods and Results: Agency website, Challenge.gov, direct e-mails to Biomedical Engineering Departments, listserv, press release, and word of mouth.

Incentives: $10,000 cash prize purse, along with up to $2,000 reimbursement to travel to award ceremony for the winner in each of the three categories. Also, two honorable mentions in each of three challenge categories.

Evaluation: Nine judges from the NIH with relevant backgrounds evaluated the entries for significance of the problem addressed, impact on potential users, innovative nature of design, and the evidence of a working prototype.

Partnerships: Challenge organizers have collaborated with the Biomedical Engineering Society to incorporate an award ceremony for their challenge within their annual meeting and the National Collegiate Inventors and Innovators Alliance (NCIIA) to announce DEBUT to their stakeholders via their websites and listservs.

Resources: Agency resources directed to the challenge, other than the cash prizes described above, consist of personnel, including the Challenge Manager; the senior leadership of NIBIB who provide guidance; scientific staff who contribute to the evaluation of the entries; and technical staff who manage the website. Funding for execution of the challenge was allocated under NIBIB's appropriation account.

Results: DEBUT generated a lot of excitement among Biomedical Engineering departments and students, as well as those in life sciences, and other areas of engineering and computer science. Challenge organizers received 61 entries from 39 different universities with 284 students involved in the projects submitted. Most of the entries were of very high quality. In addition to engaging students in increasingly sophisticated design projects, the challenge served to introduce the next generation of biomedical engineers to the NIBIB.

4.13.   Now Trending: #Health in My Community

Overview: Studies show that social media trends can be powerful indicators of community health issues. With early identification, health officials can respond quickly and educate the public on how to protect their health and minimize the spread of the disease, therein enhancing individual and community resilience and potentially preventing a public health emergency, such as a pandemic. The Office of the Assistant Secretary for Preparedness and Response (ASPR) challenged participants, from university students to large companies, to create a web-based application that analyzes open source Twitter data for health topics and delivers "Top 5 Trending Illnesses" outputs for both a specified geographic area and the national level. This challenge was created in response to a request from state and local health officials to have an easy-to-use application that makes social media a useful information source for health.

Website:
http://challenge.gov/HHS/334-now-trending-health-in-my-community

Problem Statement: Studies are showing that trending topics on social media can serve as an early indicator and warning of emerging health issues within a community. This challenge offered the opportunity for an individual or team to showcase their skills at the national level while helping to advance the field of health analytics. Specifically, this challenge asked participants to create a web-based application that analyzes open source Twitter data for health topics and delivers "Top 5 Trending Illnesses" outputs for both a specified geographic area and the national level.

Goal: Improve health surveillance and situational awareness.

Why a Prize as Preferred Method: Due to the focus of the challenge being a newer area of study, ASPR believed that a challenge would be a good way to be able to tap into innovative minds outside of traditional contracting routes in order to create a useful and forward thinking tool for health officials.

Participants: ASPR hoped to have a variety of entrants to this challenge, from academia to companies to private citizens. The competition had 33 total entries with teams and individuals that came from all different backgrounds. Thirteen entries were from companies (both large and small), ten were from academia, six were private individuals, and four were private teams. The entries were from all areas of the country.

Timeline:
Solicitation Open – 3/16/2012
Solicitation Close – 6/1/2012
Winners Announced – 9/13/2012

Solicitation and Outreach Methods and Results: ASPR used a multifaceted marketing plan that included social media, email, presentations before key stakeholder and target participant groups, and outreach through HHS leadership. Social media and referral from friends/colleagues turned out to be the most successful outreach methods.

Incentives: App developer presentation at the ASPR FUSION Bring Your Own Data Citizen Science Conference; $21,000 in prize money; $1,000 toward travel to conference from ASPR OPEO operating budget.

Evaluation: ASPR used a panel of technical advisors to initially review the entries. These advisors represented all the areas that this competition touched: health, social media, and technology. The technical advisors reviewed the entries and provided their feedback to ASPR for consideration. Participant entries were judged on their application's accessibility from multiple platforms and for users of all ability levels, the application's innovation, user interface, and potential to impact health situational awareness. The challenge judge, Dr. Nicole Lurie, selected the ultimate winner. Challenge organizers felt the use of technical advisors form specific industries was an effective way to approach a competition that has a reach into multiple disciplines.

Partnerships: None

Resources: The competition was created and administered by the Fusion Cell, an office within ASPR. This required the full time efforts of one employee (Challenge Manager) and part time efforts of two others in the office. To assist with challenge management, the services of MetroStar Systems, Inc. were procured via the GSA 541.4G schedule.

Results: Since the close of the competition, the winning technology has been used by health departments from the local to the Federal level. State and local departments have used the website and its information to inform the health situational awareness of their populations, as an indication of where public health messaging is needed, and to build a baseline of health information in social media for better identification of anomalies in data. At the Federal level, the website was used in both the Hurricane Isaac and Hurricane Sandy response in order to track health trends in affected populations.

4.14. 2012 Surgeon General's Video Contest: Tobacco- I'm Not Buying It

Overview: The Surgeon General's (SG) Video Contest for Youth and Young Adults invited young Americans to speak up about tobacco and tell us why they are "not buying it." In conjunction with the 2012 Surgeon General's Report, "Preventing Tobacco Use among Youth and Young Adults", the Centers for Disease Control (CDC) challenged youth aged 13-17 and young adults ages 18-25 to develop original videos that featured one or more of the report findings.

Website:
http://2012sgr.challenge.gov/ or
http://www.cdc.gov/tobacco/data_statistics/sgr/2012/contest/

Problem Statement: Tobacco use by youth, teens, and young adults remains shockingly high in the United States. The 2012 Surgeon General's Report highlighted the health impacts of tobacco use and how the tobacco industry targets youth through advertising, promotional activities, and manipulation of peer group influences.

Goal: Public education

Why a Prize as Preferred Method: Using a prize competition provided the ability to promote the 2012 SG's report in a way that engaged the target audiences where and how they communicate: online, via social networks, and through user-generated content like video. Youth and young adults are the leading creators and viewers of online video content, and the challenge allowed the CDC to disseminate key messages from the SG's report through peer-to-peer communication. Over 80% of social media users trust their peers more than they do a company or brand so incentivizing youth people to learn about the findings in the report and communicate the key messages in their own voice and style was a must for this report focused solely on youth and young adults. The winning videos continue to be featured, viewed, and shared from the CDC's website and social media profiles including YouTube, Facebook, and Twitter.

Participants: Youth and young adults, ages 13-25. OSH received a total of 85 video submissions, of which 63 met the challenge criteria.

Timeline:
Solicitation Open – 3/8/2012
Solicitation Close – 4/22/2012
Winners Announced – 5/30/2012

Solicitation and Outreach Methods and Results: OSH engaged youth advocacy partners and the general public through traditional and social media channels to encourage submissions and voting for the finalists in each category.

Incentives: Winning videos were announced by U.S. Surgeon General and promoted on YouTube and CDC.gov. A total of $10,000 was divided among the 4 categories. A $1,000 grand prize and three $500 runner-up prizes were awarded for the middle/high school competition (both English and Spanish categories) and the young adult/college competition (both English and Spanish categories). Upon selection of the winning videos by an expert panel, all 10 winning videos were featured on CDC's website, promoted via earned and social media and live on CDC's YouTube channel.

Evaluation: Submissions were initially screened for the required criteria, described below, by a panel of CDC staff. The eligible videos were then uploaded to YouTube, and the general public voted for their favorites in the four (two age-based categories for both English and Spanish submissions) categories based on the following challenge criteria: creativity; use of the one or more key SG Report findings; and use or inclusion of the official SGR website. The top 10 submissions in each category from the public voting were then judged by an expert panel made up of Federal and national tobacco prevention and control partners.

Partnerships: Key partnerships were leveraged to ensure the success of the Surgeon General's Video challenge. Officially, challenge organizers worked closely with the Surgeon General's office and tobacco prevention and control partners and grantees to engage youth advocacy groups in their states and communities. Non-traditional partners played a key role in the success of the challenge, as challenge organizers engaged educational institutions, youth ministries, and other youth groups across the country. This outreach to non-traditional partners to promote the challenge resulted in an increased number of challenge entries.

Resources: Prize money was funded through an ICF contract. The total amount of prize money allocated was $10,000, of which $9,000 in prize money was awarded. A minimal amount of ICF contract hours were used to develop marketing materials.

Results: Through this competition, OSH was able to focus on youth tobacco prevention and promote the release of the 2012 Surgeon General's report. Using video as a creative outlet, young people personally engaged with the report findings and educated their peers about the dangers of tobacco use. Winners were interviewed by local newspapers and asked to perform their songs or show their videos at their local high schools, churches, and events. Tobacco prevention and control partners with winners from their states have requested copies of their videos to show in presentations and for their web and social media efforts. The U.S. Surgeon General has featured winning videos in her talks and presentations about the 2012 Surgeon General's report, since she officially announced the winners during a live Twitter chat in May of 2012. All videos can be viewed from the CDC Office on Smoking and Health competition web page.[46]

---

[46] http://www.cdc.gov/tobacco/data_statistics/sgr/2012/contest/#vote

4.15.   Surgeon General's Healthy Apps Challenge

Overview: The U.S. Surgeon General's Healthy Apps Challenge encouraged the development and submission of technology applications that will complement and enhance two key aspects of the Surgeon General's prevention agenda: The Surgeon General's Vision for a Healthy and Fit Nation[47] and the nation's first National Prevention Strategy.[48] Specifically, the challenge highlighted the ability of new technologies to: (1) provide health information tailored to the needs of the user; and (2) empower users (the general public) to regularly engage in and enjoy health-promoting behaviors related to fitness and physical activity, nutrition and healthy eating, and physical, mental and emotional well-being. This challenge was conducted in collaboration with ONC.

Website: http://sghealthyapps.challenge.gov/

Problem Statement: Non-communicable diseases such as cardiovascular disease, cancer, and chronic respiratory disease account for a large majority of deaths in the United States. The links between unhealthy behaviors (e.g., physical inactivity, unhealthy eating, tobacco use, excessive alcohol use) and these chronic illnesses have been well established. The Surgeon General's Vision for a Healthy and Fit Nation and the National Prevention Strategy both highlight the importance of health behaviors in preventing disease and creating a healthy and fit nation. The National Prevention Strategy further envisions a prevention-oriented society where all sectors recognize the value of health for individuals, families, and society and work together to achieve better health for all Americans. The National Prevention Strategy also emphasizes the importance of empowering individuals with tools and information to make healthy choices and shifting the focus of the nation's health to prevention and integrated wellness (i.e., physical, behavioral, social, and emotional health), rather than focusing primarily on illness and disease. National public health recommendations and guidelines currently exist for physical activity;[49] nutrition,[50] and overall health and wellness.[51] Yet, currently, approximately 40 percent of American adults report that they do not engage in any leisure-time physical activity, with less than half the population meeting public health recommendations for physical activity. In 2009, fewer than 1 in 10 Americans included the recommended amounts of fruit and vegetables in their diet. Over one-third of Americans are currently obese. Research also finds that sleep health contributes to obesity and disease, but 40 percent of Americans report unintentionally falling asleep during the day at least once in the preceding month.

---

[47] http://www.surgeongeneral.gov/initiatives/walking/index.html
[48] http://www.surgeongeneral.gov/initiatives/prevention/strategy/national-prevention-strategy-fact-sheet.pdf
[49] Physical Activity Guidelines for Americans: http://www.health.gov/paguidelines/
[50] MyPlate: http://www.choosemyplate.gov/
[51] Healthy People 2020: http://www.healthypeople.gov/2020/default.aspx

Goal: Encourage the development (by innovators) and use (by everyday Americans) of consumer-facing technology to create a healthy and fit nation.

Why a Prize as Preferred Method: A competition offers an excellent way to reach the people and businesses that are involved in application development and to encourage them to submit their apps for evaluation. The built-in publicity and organization provided through the Challenge.gov site means that the resources of a small office could be maximized. Challenge organizers' office has no available resources to offer prize money, so the attraction for those who entered was the publicity involved.

Participants: Developers, designers, and entrepreneurs. 56 teams submitted apps ranging from those help individuals to track their health promoting behaviors to locators that identify services that can improve health or reinforce healthful outcomes.

Timeline:
Solicitation Open – 12/6/2011
Solicitation Closed – 12/31/2011
Winners Announced – 2/22/2012

Solicitation and Outreach Methods and Results: Social media (Twitter) and outreach to new media community through promotion at conferences and in keynote speeches.

Incentives: No cash prize purses were offered for this competition. Winners and those highly recommended are highlighted in media release (February 17, 2012) and on the Surgeon General's website.[52]

Evaluation: In the first round, ONC contractors assessed the eligibility of submissions on the basis of essential requirements: acceptable platform; functionality; available free; no requirements for additional purchases or equipment. In the second round of evaluations, each app was evaluated by at least two people from within HHS with relevant technical and policy expertise. The top 15 submissions were then sent to high-profile internal and external assessors for evaluation; again, each application received two separate evaluations. The stringent HHS requirements imposed on external judges really precluded their use in the formal sense.

Partnerships: None

---

[52] http://www.surgeongeneral.gov/news/pressreleases/sg_healthy_app_challenge-winners.html

Resources: The only costs incurred by the Office of the Surgeon General under this Challenge were those for the Federal Register Notice and the time of a senior policy staff person. Additional resources and time were provided by ONC through i2.

Results: 72 eligible entries were received, and mostly of high standard. The Surgeon General's ability to embrace new technologies, use them to encourage people to be more engaged in healthy activities, and show how they can help people make healthy choices all help drive awareness of key OSG and HHS initiatives such as prevention, obesity, tobacco, healthy eating, and physical activity. The winning app in one category needed to addresses both exercise and healthy eating. The winning Lose It! app helps users achieve diet and exercise goals by setting a daily calorie budget and recording food intake and exercise to meet that budget. Users can invite friends to view logs on Facebook to boost motivation and encourage one another. Two other apps in this category received high marks. Fit Friendzy is an app that encourages everyone to be more active by highlighting the benefits of not just traditional exercise, but also of tasks like gardening, dancing, housecleaning, and snow shoveling, allowing users to challenge themselves or join in challenges with friends. There is also the option to share exercise data with health care providers. The MapMyFitness app encompasses both fitness and nutrition education, using built-in GPS of mobile devices to track fitness activities. Users can establish a training log, record activity, keep track of calories consumed, and share information with friends. The winner in a second category needed to encourage people to develop healthy habits, make positive changes in their lives, and stick with them. The winning Healthy Habits app recognizes that good health is not just about keeping active and eating healthily, but also about getting a good night's sleep, thinking positively, and spending time with family and friends. It also addresses health issues such as smoking, wearing sunscreen, taking time for creative activities, and reducing stress. Users can choose which healthy habits to track. Two additional apps focused on children's health received high marks. Max's Plate is an app that educates young children and their parents about healthy eating and provides a fun and entertaining way to learn about good nutrition. Short Sequence: Kids' Yoga Journey is an app that has simple instructions for yoga poses for children and beautiful illustrations.

4.16.   Seeing My World through a Safer Lens Video Challenge

Overview: In commemoration of the 20th Anniversary of the CDC National Center for Injury Prevention and Control (Injury Center), challenge organizers hosted a video competition to answer the question, "What does Injury and Violence Prevention Look Like in My Community?" The "Seeing My World through a Safer Lens" video competition asked injury and violence professionals, students, and the general public to create a short video that shows injury and violence prevention in their neighborhood, community, state, or region. This competition provided a community/local perspective on prevention of the leading cause of death among Americans under the age of 44. By drawing attention to how others are working in their communities to prevent violence and injuries, challenge organizers can change the perspective that injuries are not just random "accidents," but rather a preventable public health issue. The "Seeing My World through a Safer Lens" video competition asks injury and violence professionals, students, and the general public to create a short video that shows injury and violence prevention in their neighborhood, community, state, or region.

Website:
saferlens.challenge.gov

Problem Statement: Through personalized videos, challenge entrants showed how proven prevention strategies are being implemented in various forms of communities. By showcasing the winning videos in each category of submission (Student View, General Public View, and Injury and Violence Professional View), the challenge was highlighted steps for injury and violence prevention. The participants were asked to create a 90 second video that answered the question, "What does injury and violence prevention look like in my community?" Entrants were required to choose from a selected list of injury and violence topics to showcase one prevention strategy or the impact of injuries or violence where they live.

Goal: Public education

Why a Prize as Preferred Method: In order to reach the general public population and engage students, a small cash prize ($500/ category) was offered to incentivize populations that are not already engaged in public health conversations around violence and injury prevention. In order to gain a broader perspective from local injury and violence professionals that do not have the means or programs to compete for structured contracts, they were also eligible for a cash prize.

Participants: The "Seeing My World through a Safer Lens" video competition reached out to partner organizations, violence and injury prevention professionals, student organizations, and the general public for submissions into the competition. In total there were 54 submitted videos, 25 of which adhered to all of the rules and video eligibility criteria by the final submission date. The final 25 videos were judged in three categories violence and injury prevention professionals (10 videos), students (9 videos), and general public (6 videos).

Timeline:
Solicitation Open – 5/1/2012
Solicitation Close – 7/31/2012
Winners Announced – 9/10/2012

Solicitation and Outreach Methods and Results: The promotion of the "Seeing My World though a Safer Lens" video competition included: social media outreach; listserv and GovD email announcements to key partners and constituents; online promotion; and direct outreach to partner organization for inclusion in their websites and announcements. Other organizations and student affiliates were solicited for assistance in promotion, such as APHA student organizations and national schools of public health.

Incentives: Each submission category (injury and violence prevention professional, student, and general public) had an award of $500; $1,500 in total.

Evaluation: The submissions from the video competition were judged by a panel of 12 judges, consisting of CDC Injury Center leadership, topic-specific subject matter experts, communications staff, and leaders in partner agencies (the Safe States Alliance and National Public Health Information Council). These judges scored each video against the weighted judging criteria (creativity, use of injury or violence prevention topic, communication of positive prevention message, length, and audio and video quality).

Partnerships: No formal partnerships were initiated for the "Seeing My World through a Safer Lens" challenge. However, a number of grantees and partners agreed to share messaging and promotion of the competition.

Resources: Funds were allocated from program funds dedicated to activities for commemoration of the Injury Center's 20th anniversary.

Results: The goal of the "Seeing My World through a Safer Lens" video competition is to increase public education about how violence and injuries are preventable. As a leading cause of death for people under the age of 44, the competition aimed to allow people to see how people are implementing scientifically-based prevention strategies where they live, work, or play. The video competition resulted in advancing the Injury Center's vision of preventing violence and injuries and their consequences, by moving from science into action. By bringing together a diverse group of people, invested in stopping injuries and violence and their associated consequences, the video competition succeeded in showing that CDC's science-based approaches can be implemented at any level, within any environment. These winning videos will be used as examples of how digital technology, social media, and social sharing can set an example for positive communications messaging around injury and violence topic areas.

4.17.   Million Hearts Caregiver Video Challenge

Overview: CDC and Prevention and the Million Hearts™ initiative invited family caregivers to participate in a video competition that offered $1,000 in prize money. Million Hearts™ is a five-year initiative launched by the Department of Health and Human Services with a goal of preventing one million heart attacks and strokes in the United States over the next five years. CDC and Million Hearts™ invited people who help to prevent or control high blood pressure or maintain the heart health of a loved one to share their stories of care giving by creating short, original videos. The videos showed the variety of ways a caregiver contributes to another person's heart health and provided helpful tips related to high blood pressure prevention and control. The video challenge engaged the caregiver community and promoted heart disease prevention through blood pressure control, medication adherence, and lifestyle changes.

Website:
http://millionhearts.challenge.gov/

Problem Statement: Heart attack and stroke are the first and fourth leading causes of death in the United States. High blood pressure, one of the major risk factors for heart disease, can be prevented and controlled. Family caregivers play an important role in helping their loved ones prevent and control high blood pressure. The competition invited family caregivers to share their stories of care giving by creating original, compelling videos that are less than two minutes long. The videos were required to include a description of how the caregiver contributes to another person's heart health and helpful tips related to high blood pressure prevention or control.

Goal: Public education to raise awareness of the role of caregivers and family members in preventing and controlling high blood pressure.

Why a Prize as Preferred Method: In the area of health, video competitions function as a tool to promote interest and engagement in public health topics. They drive the public to present creative ideas and innovative solutions while raising awareness and educating audiences on a public health issue. The competition was a tool for Million Hearts™ to use to reach out to and interact with a key audience through a new, compelling mechanism not yet used by their initiative.

Participants: CDC hoped to mobilize family caregivers. This challenge received two eligible submissions: one from Chicago, Illinois and one from Henderson, Nevada.

Timeline:
Solicitation Open – 7/16/2012
Solicitation Close – 8/31/2012
Winners Announced – 10/8/2012

Solicitation and Outreach Methods and Results: CDC used the following methods to market the video challenge: weekly social media posts on CDC's and Million Hearts'™ Facebook and Twitter accounts, two CDC Features on CDC.gov home page, a Federal Register Notice published on July 9, a Million Hearts'™ web site home page posting, CDC's GovDelivery e-mail listserv, and postings on video competition databases (onlinevideocontests.com, filmthenext.com). Million Hearts™ also encouraged their major partners, American Heart Association and Administration on Aging, among others, to promote the competition through their social media accounts and blog web sites. Various health-related blogs published content describing the challenge and leading the public to the challenge web site. There are many likely factors that may have contributed to low participation, such as promotion efforts that did not reach the target audience, an insufficient submission period of six weeks, and discouraging criteria and standards for submissions for amateur video producers.

Incentives: The winning videos were promoted through CDC and Million Hearts social media channels. $1,000 total cash prizes funded by the CDC Foundation, an independent, non-profit organization, donated all prize money to CDC via the Outreach and Partnership Fund.

Evaluation: A panel of three judges evaluated the videos by scoring each against criteria including appropriateness, storytelling, quality of video, and potential to impact others.

Partnerships: Million Hearts™ reached out to their major public and non-profit partners for help in promoting the competition on their social media outlets and web sites. Many nonprofit, federal, and state health agencies shared social media posts on Facebook and Twitter, or shared information about the competition through blogs and web sites. CDC also partnered with the CDC Foundation, which donated prize money.

Resources: Some personnel time. Prize purse was donated by the CDC Foundation, graphics were created in-house, and free marketing channels were used.

Results: The competition web site and subsequent online marketing materials were written to present the requirements for submissions, to encourage participation, and to educate the public on the Million Hearts™ initiative and heart disease prevention. Results from tracking social media activity show these posts led over 2,500 people to the competition web site throughout the submission period from July 16 to August 31, 2012. These social media messages, viewed by over a hundred thousand "followers" of CDC social media, were often shared by other Federal agencies and national partners who have thousands of their own followers. Despite the low number of submissions, the winning videos successfully provided tips on how to prevent and control high blood pressure and described the role of a family caregiver. The first place winner, in particular, used an innovative approach through motion info-graphics to describe how a caregiver helps a loved one maintain their heart health.

5. Department of Labor

5.1. Equal Pay App Challenge

Overview: The National Equal Pay Task Force and DOL engaged innovators, educators, and IT developers to help build innovative tools to educate the public about the gender pay gap and promote equal pay for women.

Website:
http://equalpay.challenge.gov/

Problem Statement: Nearly 50 years after President Kennedy signed the Equal Pay Act, women are still paid less than their male counterparts for doing comparable jobs. This pay gap means that each time the average woman starts a new job, she's likely to start from a lower base salary, and that, over time, the pay gap between her and her male colleagues is likely to grow. For the average working woman, the pay gap means she will receive $150 less in her weekly paycheck, $8,000 less at the end of the year, and $380,000 less over her lifetime. For women of color and women with disabilities, the disparity is even bigger.

Goal: DOL wanted to engage leaders in academia, non-profit organizations, industry innovators, IT professionals, and other equal pay supporters to use publicly available labor data and other online resources to educate users about the pay gap and develop tools to promote equal pay. DOL's four primary goals were to provide greater access to pay data by gender, race, and ethnicity; provide tools for early career coaching; improve education on negotiation; and promote online mentoring.

Why a Prize as Preferred Method: DOL employed a prize competition to tap into the pools of talented developers, educators, innovators, and industry leaders from across the country who traditionally do not participate in Government IT development or mission-specific exercises. Challenge organizers wanted to collaborate directly with new and established innovators that typically do not participate as traditional stakeholders.

Participants: DOL wanted to collaborate with people who participate in creating new, groundbreaking online platforms and technologies, and are experts in developing mobile applications. The DOL Equal Pay App Challenge was supported by over 1,500 individuals, received 12 qualified submissions, and resulted in seven winners.

Solicitation and Outreach Methods and Results: DOL utilized the Challenge.gov platform to host and launch the DOL Equal Pay App competition. The Department used multiple methods to market the challenge, including press releases and social media. Additionally, DOL created a dedicated website, http://developer.dol.gov/, which housed APIs, SDKs and sample code for multiple platforms to ensure developer success.

Incentives: All prizes offered to winners originated from non-Federal entities.

Evaluation: DOL's evaluation process was composed of internal and external evaluation panels and included five evaluation drivers: (1) Creativity, innovation, and ease of use; (2) Promotion of access to important data and resources; (3) Usability by users with different skill sets and language preferences; (4) Consideration of partnerships that will ensure sustainability of the app; and (5) Ability to reach a variety of audiences.

Partnerships: The challenge was developed and executed through an internal partnership among DOL component agencies. Private sector partners included Women

Innovate Mobile, Carnegie Mellon University, Google, The Daily Muse, Salary.com, Interview Street and the Massachusetts Institute of Technology (MIT).

Resources: Resources used for the development, execution, and management of the competition included staff time.

Results: The Equal Pay App Challenge on Challenge.gov advanced DOL's mission by leveraging existing program information, technology, and public innovation to raise awareness on equal pay and provide effective tools for employers and employees. The competition amplified the Equal Pay Taskforce's mission on wage equality by expanding the amount of quality online tools, effective messaging and partnerships with non-traditional stakeholders in the academic and digital spectrum. The competition was featured on multiple media outlets including Forbes, The Daily Muse, New York Times, and Sacramento Bee, in addition to other online publications and mainstream blogs.

5.2. Disability Employment App Challenge

Overview: The competition asked developers to help build innovative tools to improve employment opportunities and outcomes for people with disabilities.

Website:
http://disability.challenge.gov/

Problem Statement: Nearly twenty-two years after the passage of the Americans with Disabilities Act and thirty-nine years after the passage of the Rehabilitation Act of 1973 – two of the most significant disability employment-related pieces of legislation in American history – people with disabilities continue to be employed at much lower levels than the general population. Not only do people with disabilities have a significantly higher unemployment rate than the general population, they also have a much lower labor force participation rate. According to the most recent data from the Department of Labor's Bureau of Labor Statistics (April 2012), people with disabilities had a 20.3% labor force participation rate compared to 69.1% for their non-disabled peers, and people with disabilities had an unemployment rate of 12.5% compared to 7.6% for their non-disabled peers. For minorities with disabilities, these disparities are even greater. This represents a significant loss of willing and able talent to the American workforce, loss of income for people without jobs, and economic loss to the country.

Goal: DOL wanted to leverage technology in innovative ways to promote recruitment resources for employers, develop job-training and skill-building tools for job seekers, facilitate employment-related transportation options, and expand web and Information Communication Technology (ICT) accessibility.

Why a Prize as Preferred Method: DOL employed a prize competition to tap into the pools of talented developers across the country that traditionally do not participate in government IT development or mission-specific exercises. Challenge organizers wanted to collaborate directly with new and established innovators that typically do not participate as traditional stakeholders.

Participants: DOL wanted to collaborate with people who participate in creating new, groundbreaking online platforms and technologies, and are experts in developing mobile applications. The DOL Disability Employment App Challenge was supported by over 2,400 individuals and received over 30 submissions.

Solicitation and Outreach Methods and Results: DOL utilized Challenge.gov to host and launch the DOL Disability Employment App competition. The Department used multiple methods to market the challenge, including press releases and social media via its Open Government Blog and Facebook and Twitter accounts. DOL additionally created a dedicated website, http://developer.dol.gov/, that housed APIs, SDKs and sample code for multiple platforms to ensure developer success.

Incentives: Competition prizes were offered in monetary form and as invitations to the FCC developer event, "Developing with Accessibility," in Washington, DC on September 6 – 7th, 2012. The prizes awarded totaled $10,000: a first place prize of $5,000; a second place prize of $3,000; and a third place prize of $2,000.

Evaluation: A two-phase judging process assessed submissions against several criteria: (1) alignment with mission, (2) creativity, (3) ease of use, (4) provided access to important data and resources, (5) attractive users with different skill sets and language preferences, (6) accessibility, (7) partnerships, and (8) audiences targeted. The final judging panel was made up of DOL, the Department of Education, Social Security Administration, and private sector industry leaders including IBM, Craig Newmark, and the Assistive Technology Industry Association (ATIA).

Partnerships: The challenge was developed and executed through an internal partnership between DOL component agencies. Challenge organizers also partnered with the U.S. Department of Education and U.S. Social Security Administration. Private sector partners included IBM, ATIA, and Craig Newmark.

Resources: Resources used for the development, execution, and management of this competition included staff time various DOL component agencies.

Results: The DOL Disability Employment App Challenge on Challenge.gov advanced DOL's mission by leveraging existing technology and public innovation to raise public awareness about disability employment tools for employers and employees, including employer compliance with federal workplace laws, speech augmentation tools, 508 compliant applications, and disability-focused job boards. Three prizes were awarded, one in each of the following categories: innovation, public voting, and accessibility. A description of each winner is below:

- Innovation Award Winner: Access Jobs. Access Jobs is a job search portal specifically designed for job seekers with disabilities. The website implements usable accessibility techniques, such as responsive design, which allow the website to be experienced in the same way across all platforms.
- The People's Choice Award Winner: VoisPal – Speak as You Think! VoisPal is an Android-based Augmentative and Alternative Communication (AAC) app designed to help people with speech difficulties.
- Above and Beyond Accessibility Award Winner: AccDC: Accelerated Dynamic Content. AccDC is a scalable, cross-browser and cross-platform compatible Dynamic Content Management System that automates the rendering of dynamic content to ensure accessibility for screen reader and keyboard only users.

6. Department of State

6.1. Innovations in Arms Control Challenge

Overview: A smaller, faster-paced world is changing the security landscape, and these changes will bring with them new challenges and evolutions in current threats. To respond to these changes, the Department of State must adapt instruments of statecraft to bring to bear the networks, technologies, and human potential of their increasingly inter-dependent and interconnected world. In this spirit, on August 28, 2012, the Department of State launched the *Innovation in Arms Control Challenge* asking Americans: "How Can the Crowd Support Arms Control Transparency Efforts?" Challenge organizers invited America to share their ideas on ways commonly available technologies can support arms control policy. Challenge organizers see great value in incorporating innovative ideas across the whole spectrum of their arms control initiatives. As the Department of State looks to the future of arms control, new thinking to face the challenges of the 21st century is vital to their success, keeping in mind the big challenges that come about as challenge organizers move to reduce nuclear weapons to lower numbers, and look for ways to monitor smaller units of account, such as chemical munitions in storage facilities.

Website:
http://www.state.gov/t/avc/innovationcompetition/index.htm
http://challenge.gov/State/394-innovation-in-arms-control-challenge

Problem Statement: How Can the Crowd Support Arms Control Transparency Efforts? This challenge asked for creative ideas from the general public to use commonly available devices to help confirm whether states are complying with treaties or international arrangements addressing weapons and nonproliferation. Treaties or international arrangements addressing weapons, nonproliferation, and confidence-building measures are generally known as "arms control." They are diplomatic tools that governments use to regulate weapons (especially weapons of mass destruction), or to increase transparency, predictability, and stability. These treaties or international arrangements support mutual security and stability in general, however, in some situations one or more parties may be motivated to violate these arms control provisions, commonly understood as "cheating." This broad challenge question was an "Ideation Challenge," formulated to obtain access to new ideas, similar to a global brainstorm for producing a breakthrough idea or market survey which may include ideas for a new product line, a new commercial application for a current product, or even a viral marketing idea to recruit new customers. Solvers were asked to provide ideas that included a description of the proposed mechanism or idea to support arms control transparency efforts; rationale for why the proposed idea will work in the real world; and any supporting information, publications, real-world use cases, or examples that reinforce the validity of the proposed idea.

Goal: The primary objective of the challenge was to discover new approaches and ideas on ways commonly available technologies can support arms control policy, to bolster interest in the general public on arms control issues, and to stimulate useful outside thinking that could provide additional transparency and information related to compliance with arms control, nonproliferation, and disarmament regimes.

Why a Prize as Preferred Method: Prize competitions can stimulate attention and encourage innovation in a highly leveraged and results-focused way. Incentives improve the performance of problem-solvers and mobilize new talent and ideas.

Participants: This challenge asked for creative ideas from across the general public, from garage tinkerers and technologists, to gadget entrepreneurs and students, to support the U.S. arms control and nonproliferation agenda. 565 registered solvers submitted 67 solutions. Of the solvers who registered, 24 were from universities including Georgetown, MIT, Princeton, Brown, Cornell, Carnegie Mellon, Stanford, UC Berkeley, Iowa State, and University of Michigan.

Although participation was limited to U.S. Citizens and permanent residents under the America COMPETES authority, challenge organizers received a lot of interest and positive feedback from foreign publics. While continuously working to achieve their Department's overall mission of international engagement, challenge organizers discovered an inability to locate the appropriate authority to engage international publics on prize incentive challenges. For future Department of State prize incentive challenges, challenge organizers are considering using existing procurement or grant authority language in order to carry out the Department of State's overall mission of engaging foreign publics while also soliciting innovative proposals that could aid the U.S. government by providing additional transparency and information related to compliance with existing or future arms control, nonproliferation and disarmament regimes. An amendment to the reauthorization of the America COMPETES Act could help alleviate the restrictions on engaging foreign publics under the existing authority.

This would facilitate the Department of State's ability to reach out to an international audience of potential competition participants.

Timeline:
Challenge Open – 08/28/12
Challenge Close – 10/26/12

Solicitation and Outreach Methods and Results: On August 28, 2012, the U.S. Department of State issued an official announcement on the Federal Register and sent out a press release on the Innovation in Arms Control Challenge. Rose Gottemoeller, Acting Under Secretary of State for Arms Control and International Security, also posted about the challenge on the Department's official blog and the White House's Office of Science and Technology Policy's blog.[53] These releases were further amplified through various social media channels inside and outside the Administration. Acting Under Secretary Gottemoeller participated in an interview with Popular Mechanics and CNN about the competition and later received wide attention. The announcement of the State Department challenge was also picked up by regional television and newspaper outlets, including the Washington Post.

Incentives: The awards will be paid to the best submission(s) as solely determined by the State Department. The total payout will be $10,000, with at least one award being no smaller than $5,000 and no award being smaller than $1,000.

Evaluation: Solutions will be reviewed in two rounds of technical reviews. After analyzing the technical reviews, finalists will be chosen by a small coordination group based on their composite weighted score. The Judging Criteria was organized into the following three categories: applicability, feasibility, and supporting documentation.

Partnerships: None

Resources: The prize challenge was funded from the Department of State's External Research Board (REB) on behalf of the Under Secretary of State for Arms Control and International Security.

Results: The competition was still open as of the end of FY 2012, so the final results of the competition will be reported in the FY 2013 prizes report to Congress. To date, the Challenge has brought more awareness of arms control issues to the American public, particularly on the challenge's focus on the applicability of commonly available devices and social networking tools to arms control policy.

---

[53] http://www.whitehouse.gov/blog/2012/09/05/challengegov-two-years-and-200-prizes-later

7. Small Business Administration

7.1. Small Business Week Video Contest

Overview: In celebration of National Small Business Week 2012, the SBA sought creative videos from small businesses that showed how they had been assisted by an SBA program or service (counseling, training, guaranteed loans, government contracts, disaster recovery, etc.). The video competition showcased amazing small businesses across the country. These businesses are creating jobs and the next big products that will help keep America competitive.

Website:
http://smallbizvid.challenge.gov/

Problem Statement: For most entrepreneurs and small businesses, the Federal government has useful programs and services, but small businesses often do not know that these programs are available.

Goal: To educate the public about how SBA programs and services help entrepreneurs and small business owners start, grow, and succeed.

Why a Prize as Preferred Method: Through Challenge.gov, SBA was able to collect video success stories at zero cost to the agency.

Participants: The competition was opened to SBA-assisted small businesses in the United States and its territories including, but not limited to, Puerto Rico, the U. S. Virgin Islands and Guam. The business owner(s) must have been a U.S. citizen or permanent resident and be at least 18 years old to enter and win. Small businesses must have met SBA's size standards and must have used at least one SBA program or service.

Timeline: The challenge was launched on April 16, 2012. The video submission deadline was May 15, 2012. The judging process was from May 16-19, 2012. The winners were announced and the challenge concluded on May 23, 2012.

Solicitation and Outreach Methods and Results:
SBA marketed the challenge successfully through social media (Twitter and Facebook), mail marketing (GovDelivery), and press releases/news advisories.

Incentives: Winning videos were shown during a Google+ Hangout hosted by SBA and the White House with SBA Administrator Karen Mills on May 23, 2012. The winners were invited to participate in the Hangout with Administrator Mills.

Evaluation: SBA's successful evaluation criteria included: length, format, educational content, story, reference to SBA program or services, and originality.

Partnerships: SBA and the White House cohosted the winners announcement.

Resources: There were no funding costs associated with this challenge. The resources SBA used included staff time.

Results: The SBA received 103 video submissions. Of those 103 videos, 73 were eligible. SBA posted the eligible videos at www.sba.gov/stories to illustrate to the public how SBA programs and services help entrepreneurs and small businesses.

7.2. Apps for Entrepreneurs Competition

Overview: The Apps for Entrepreneurs Competition challenged individuals or teams to create apps to help small businesses and entrepreneurs navigate the Federal government more efficiently.

Website:
http://entrepreneurs.challenge.gov/

Problem Statement: For most entrepreneurs and small businesses, the Federal government has useful programs and services, but it can be hard to identify, engage, and navigate Federal websites. Often, small businesses do not know that the Federal government already offers a program that they would find useful. Entrepreneurs and small businesses need better tools to navigate the Federal government's vast resources – including programs, services, and procurement opportunities. Eligible entrants were asked to create apps to help small businesses and entrepreneurs navigate the Federal Government more efficiently.

Goal: The Apps for Entrepreneurs Competition was an SBA initiative to help make Federal government programs and information more useful to small businesses. The Competition provided recognition to individuals or teams of individuals for developing innovative applications designed for the Web, a personal computer, a mobile handheld device, console, or any platform broadly accessible on the open internet that utilize data which is freely available on Federal government websites.

Why a Prize as Preferred Method: For the SBA, it was important to test and validate the challenge concept with open government data. While contracts and grants may have been great for targeted work, the challenge platform was seen as an opportunity to encourage innovation from the developer community on ideas that the SBA.gov team could further develop into useful features for their current web properties.

Participants: The agency hoped to mobilize entrepreneurs to build apps that were relevant to their own communities with business data. Geographic distribution of submissions was broad. Generally, the participants were either independent, freelance developers, or small firms that wanted to showcase their expertise.

Timeline: Challenge opened 11/05/11; closed 11/20/11; winners announced 11/23/11

Solicitation and Outreach Methods and Results: The Agency used traditional marketing channels/tactics – including blog posts, social media outreach, and press releases. Additionally, SBA entered into a contract with a local firm to create a hackathon to bring together developers to experiment with ideas for apps. SBA also worked with others in the developer community to spread the word via email list and other relevant channels.

Incentives: There were seven prizes available: one $5,000 gift card; three $3,000 gift cards; and three $2,000 gift cards. The total value of the monetary prizes was $20,000.

Evaluation: The Judging panel was composed of 10 individuals with expertise in technology, small business, and entrepreneurship from both the public and private sectors. The Judging panel evaluated the screened submissions based these criteria: use of required data; technical implementation; mission and impact; and creativity.

Partnerships: None

Resources: Staff time, and about $50K in contractor resources, including the prize purse.

Results: The challenge roughly 30 valid submissions. The completion of the challenge was a proof-of-concept exercise, where the SBA learned how to execute other challenges.

This Appendix provides a summary of some prizes and challenges conducted in FY 2012 under agency prize authorities other than COMPETES and does not include any of the multiple prize competitions conducted under other authorities in FY 2012 or prior.

LIST OF CHALLENGES

8. **National Aeronautics and Space Administration**
   8.1. Technology Demonstration: Sample Return Robot Challenge
   8.2. Theoretical Challenge: Strain Measurement of Vectran and Kevlar Webbing
   8.3. Ideation Challenge: Big Data Challenge
   8.4. Ideation Challenge: Rice Business Plan Competition (RBPC)
   8.5. App Development: Android Electrocardiography (ECG)
   8.6. App Development: Planetary Data System Challenge
   8.7. Apps Contest/Mass Collaboration: International Space Apps Challenge
   8.8. Video Challenge: Venus Transit Video Time Capsule Challenge
   8.9. Video Challenge/ Education Challenge: Zero Robotics Challenges
   8.10. Education Challenge: NASA Great Moonbuggy Race
   8.11. Education Challenge: NASA Student Launch Projects (SLP)
   8.12. Education Challenge: Lunabotics Mining Competition
   8.13. NASA Tournament Lab
   8.14. NASA Innovation Pavilion

9. **National Institute of Standards and Technology**
   9.1. NIST SHA-3 Hash Competition

10. **Department of Defense**
    10.1. Army Challenge: Federal Virtual Worlds Challenge
    10.2. Air Force Challenges: Fuel Scrubber; Grey Data; Durable Dielectrics on Polycarbonate; Energetic Core-Nanocluster Production
    10.3. DARPA Challenges: Cash for Locating and Identifying Quick Response; Shredder

8.1 Technology Demonstration: Sample Return Robot Challenge

The NASA Sample Return Robot Challenge called upon robotics innovators to build a robot that could autonomously locate, identify, and collect a variety of samples and then return the samples to a designated point without reliance on GPS or other terrestrial navigation aids. Offering a prize permitted NASA to explore multiple solutions and to pay only for achievement of the goals.

Eleven teams registered to compete. Three were small robotics companies, two were from universities, and six were small teams of robotics enthusiasts. Competitors were required to demonstrate achievement of competition requirements according to the rules. A judging team measured the robot sample collection and retrieval performance in person at the demonstration event.

The Challenge drew novel approaches from non-traditional sources. There were no winners in 2012. The competition was also the cornerstone of a large-scale public outreach effort that attracted over 7,000 guests to the competition and provided NASA with the opportunity to educate the public on NASA robotics and Mars exploration efforts. The competition documentary podcast has been downloaded over 500,000 times and continues to be rebroadcast on NASA TV and is accessible on many online sources such as iTunes. The competition is being repeated in 2013.

8.2 Strain Measurement of Vectran and Kevlar Webbing

The NASA Strain Measurement of Vectran and Kevlar Webbing Challenge looked for a new method to measure strain on Kevlar and Vectran straps in the 25 to 125°C range. Inflatable structures are being researched as a means for long-duration human habitation in space. The structural restraint layers of the current designs are made from straps that are stitched together to form webbing. NASA performs creep tests (strain) on webbing materials of woven Vectran and Kevlar straps. Currently, a photogrammetry technique is used to determine the elongation of the test specimen. A photogrammetry technique works well at room temperature for all the straps, but at elevated temperatures, the technique only works for some of the straps. Twisting and bulging of the fibers on some samples causes the breakdown of the pattern used for photogrammetry, which results in the loss of the strain data. A technique is needed to accurately measure the strain in these samples, given the fiber movement. This challenge was instituted under NASA's contract with Innocentive. Offering a prize permitted Innocentive to explore multiple solutions and to only pay for achievement of successful solutions. Other approaches would have required selection and funding based on proposals and would have provided no assurance that payment would result in successful demonstrations. Results will not be announced until early January 2013.

8.3 Big Data Challenge

The Big Data Challenge is applying the process of Open Innovation to the goal of conceptualizing new and novel approaches to utilizing "Big Data" information sets residing in various agency silos while remaining consistent with individual United States agencies missions related to the field of health, energy, and earth sciences. NASA is collaborating with the National Science Foundation (NSF), Networking and Information Technology Research and Development (NITRD), and the DOE's Office of Science in building publicly-accessible means to access multiple disparate government data sources, some very large, to promote "Data to Knowledge to Action." The first Big Data

Challenge focused on cross cutting ideas and yielded 141 registrants, 16 total submissions, and 5 winners at $750 each. Judges for these entries came from a diverse expertise set including academia, the government and commercial companies. Each winner received a 30% bonus for using streaming data. The second Big Data Challenge focused on energy data and yielded 54 registrants, 14 total submissions, and 3 winners at $500 each. Judges for these entries came from a diverse set of places including academia, the Federal government and non-profit entities. Each winner received a 30% bonus for using streaming data. The third, ongoing Big Data Challenge is focusing on earth science data. It yielded 45 registrants and 8 total submissions.

8.4 Rice Business Plan Competition

NASA's Human Health and Performance Directorate (HH&P) at Johnson Space Center has sponsored a $20,000 prize for the past five years at the Rice Business Plan Competition, an internationally recognized student business plan competition held at Rice University in Houston, Texas. Forty-two student teams enter the competition each year. The HH&P prize focuses on new and emerging health and performance based technologies and it represents the recognition of the development of a new business, small business innovation, and the entrepreneurial spirit. Each company is commercializing a health-related technology that will improve medical care capabilities on Earth and have potential application to human spaceflight. The HH&P prize has gone to Heart Sounds, Integrated Diagnostics, GlucoGo (subsequently named LyoGo), Diagenetix, and Innovostics.

Heart Sounds is commercializing a technology that would allow the non-physician to monitor heart beats and was focused on rural and third world country pre-natal care but would have obvious application to spaceflight with non-physician crewmembers and autonomous healthcare required for exploration. Integrated Diagnostics is developing and commercializing lab on chip technology that would allow multiple laboratory tests to be done on a single sample in a very small compact analysis device with the target market being the physician's office, and portable diagnostics needs of rural healthcare and third world countries with obvious application to the in-flight diagnostics during current ISS missions as well as exploration. LyoGo is commercializing a technology that in a single use administration device allows lyophilized drugs (dried to a powder form which increases portability and shelf life) to be kept separate from the mixing solution until the time of injection. This technology overcomes measurement and mixing error by the operator or patient and is directly applicable to rural and third world country healthcare and is of interest for exploration class spaceflight missions. LyoGo now has Series A venture funding. Diagenetix, Inc. is a molecular diagnostics company that developed a platform enabling quick, gene-specific detection of pathogens without expensive or complicated instrumentation, thereby increasing the accessibility of diagnostics. The gene dart technology is very promising for real-time identification of bacterial pathogens on surfaces, water, etc. during spaceflight. Since this was developed for agriculture, the company now has a U.S. Department of Agriculture grant.

Innovostics is a for-profit social venture providing point-of-care diagnostic technologies to save patient lives around the globe. Using a unique microfluidics platform and design, tests will provide accurate, inexpensive, and rapid results with only a finger prick of blood. They are currently developing the InfectDx, a diagnostic test to differentiate between bacterial, viral, and parasitic infection.

Many ideation prizes focus on getting new ideas for existing problems. This prize example is unique from many ideation competitions in that it leverages an existing competition to draw entrepreneur's attention to NASA problems. This competition is not run on an online platform like many other ideation prizes; instead it involves in-person development and judging. The model of participating in existing business plan competitions could be compared to and considered along with online crowdsourcing approaches to identify new ideas and business plans through a prize competition.

8.5 Android Electrocardiography

The NASA Tournament Lab Mobile ECG Challenge asked competitors to design and build a mobile Android based ECG application capable of displaying and recording a 12 lead ECG signal collected via a Bluetooth signal. ECG measurements are important in diagnostic and research areas of human health both on Earth and in space. In many areas of the world and in space medical hardware is difficult to transport or obtain. Thus, NASA challenged competitors to use existing, readily available hardware platforms to develop a software application that would create a monitoring option without needing new hardware. This was a unique challenge because is required a blend of hardware and UI programming skills to participate. These combined skills sets can be difficult to find. The prize approach used for this challenge found a total of 53 registrants. Through the challenge nine entrants — who had combined skills sets that NASA might not traditionally have ready access to — provided 22 unique submissions. There were 6 total winning entries from 4 unique submitters from 3 countries. NASA is working to ready the winning solutions for Agency use.

8.6 Planetary Data System Challenge

The NASA Planetary Data System is an archive that hosts terabytes of valuable data from hundreds of data sources and spans decades of research. Data is maintained by a federation of 10 teams organized into nodes across the United States. While PDS data is available publically through its various websites, effective use requires deep familiarity with the data, data structure, and federated organization. In order to better realize the value of this national resource, PDS posted challenges through the NASA Tournament Lab on TopCoder.com in 2011 to design and build a homogenous access layer that better serves both scientists and citizens. The goals of the competition were to leverage the new PDS data access layer to develop new applications that showcase valuable PDS data and demonstrate how it could be used in scientific, educational, and social settings.

This challenge produced Android, iPad, and iPhone applications. Two applications leveraged PDS data for high school lessons, aligned to Core Curriculum standards, and one of these is an interactive Augmented Reality platform. The series also included two applications developed by high school students, one of which combined PDS data with social network themes allowing individuals to see the data their friends are looking at, and share it. The challenges enabled student engagement while producing applications that were both fun to use and novel.

8.7 International Space Apps Challenge

The International Space Apps Challenge featured 71 challenges related to how NASA explores space and improves life on Earth. The challenge was an international hackathon-style event that took place over a 48-hour period in cities on all seven continents on the weekend of April 21, 2012.

The problem statements in open hardware, open software, data visualization, and citizen science were developed from within NASA, from partner agencies and organizations, and from public submissions. Teams were encouraged to submit solutions to address any of the featured challenges, and 101 solutions were received at the end of the 48-hour global event.

The goals of the International Space Apps Challenge were to:
1. Create new technologies and approaches that can solve some of the key challenges of NASA as well as making current efforts more cost-effective (e.g., conduct science, forecast terrestrial and space weather, monitor climate change, understand earth science applications, and support disaster response and recovery).
2. Exercise a government's interest in using open data and technology, in partnership with others, to address global needs, and extend the use of space data and technology for additional applications.
3. Engage citizens in countries with little or no investments in space exploration to contribute to space exploration through open source, open data, and code development.
4. Promote Science, Technology, Engineering and Mathematics (STEM) education by encouraging students from around the world to utilize open technology for solutions to global challenges.
5. Encourage international partnership and mutual understanding.
6. Demonstrate a commitment to the principles of the Open Government Partnership.

The first International Space Apps Challenge offered seven challenges specific to satellite hardware and payloads, including submissions from at least two commercial organizations. These challenges received multiple solutions in the areas of satellite tracking, suborbital payloads, command and control systems, and leveraging commercial smartphone technology for orbital remote sensing. These were enthusiastically embraced in the wider community, particularly among the Makers.

The International Space Apps Challenge engaged a diverse group of people to contribute toward NASA's objectives of expanding human knowledge of Earth and space, improving spaceflight technology as well as making it more efficient, utilizing and extending NASA's scientific and engineering data and resources, and doing this in cooperation with other nations. The Challenge also invested in strengthening pockets of innovation, encouraging STEM utilization, and mobilizing these resources for the Administration's priorities. There were six winning apps, but the real "results" of the Challenge are a 2,000+ person community engaged in and excited about space exploration, thinking creatively and technologically, and ready to apply that experience to challenges identified by the agency, all at relatively low cost and on a short timeline.

8.8 Venus Transit Video Time Capsule Challenge

NASA challenged participants to use existing footage and create video time capsules that tell the story of this Transit to be used as a message to future citizens in 2117 as they get ready to watch the next Venus Transit. The purpose of this competition was to create a 60 second video that combines provided footage of the 2012 Venus Transit with original footage to tell an original and amazing story. The ultimate goal was to raise awareness of the historical, educational, and scientific purpose of the last Venus Transit of this generation's lifetime and to document, visually, this snapshot in time in order to provide perspective on what it was like to see it on earth in 2012.
The final deliverable from this competition produced a high quality video that serves as a video time capsule of the 2012 Venus. The first place video can be viewed here: http://tongal.com/work/4rauhc.

8.9 Zero Robotics Challenges

"Zero Robotics" (ZR) is an annual robotics programming competition where the robots are Synchronized Position Hold Engage Reorient Experimental Satellites (SPHERES) inside the International Space Station (ISS). Competitors learn, compete, and collaborate in programming the SPHERES to accomplish specific missions designed by the Zero Robotics Team at the Massachusetts Institute of Technology (MIT). After several phases of virtual competition, finalists are selected to compete in a live championship aboard the ISS. An astronaut will conduct the championship competition in microgravity with a live broadcast. While there are no prizes (other than a trophy) for the middle school and high school student competitions, two prize-based Zero Robotics competitions were conducted in 2012. First, the Zero Robotics Algorithm Challenges were open competitions conducted to develop the 2012 Zero Robotics game. Second, a promotional video was crowd-sourced using the Tongal Platform. The resulting video was propagated via social media and was the #7 viral video of the week.

The challenge of the ZR Algorithm Challenges was to build the Zero Robotics infrastructure using TopCoder crowdsourcing competitions. At a high level, the development tasks undertaken using collaborative competition were: (a) integration of a graphical editor; (b) development of the ZR community website; (c) development of the SPHERES integrated programming environment using the 2010 version as a prototype; and (4) integration of the SPHERES high-fidelity simulation into the TopCoder server compilation and testing "Farm", which is the robust back-end handling and implementing the ZR simulation requests.

The objective of the promotional video competition was to generate a commercial that would best capture the interest of the "Zero Robotics Challenge" participants who are namely students (middle and high school), parents, and teachers. This video generation competition was dived into 3 phases. In the first phase, competitions submitted short descriptions (140 characters or less) on potential video ideas. The second phase captured pitches (storyboard and text) from the various ideas generated previously. The final phase was video production and submission.

The Zero Robotics Video Challenge Top video winner and MIT video has been added to the NASA YouTube channel. These two videos were used by Brand Ads to promote Zero Robotics on online gaming sites and Social Media sites. All edited winning videos are available for ZR use on website to promote HS and MS competitions. The winning video can be found here: http://tongal.com/work/53h1g6.

8.10 NASA Great Moonbuggy Race

The 19th annual NASA Great Moonbuggy Race was held April 12-14, 2012, at the U.S. Space & Rocket Center in Huntsville, Ala. At this competition more than 70 student teams, many representing schools that field competitors year after year, demonstrated the same engineering skills and innovation that made NASA's Apollo-era lunar rover program a success four decades ago. The event challenges high school, college, and university students to design, build, and race lightweight, human-powered rovers – "Moonbuggies" – which address challenges much like those faced by NASA's lunar rover developers in the late 1960s. The annual competition is designed to teach students to troubleshoot and solve problems; to demonstrate NASA's continuing commitment to inspiring new generations of scientists, engineers, and astronauts; to provide opportunities and support systems that recruit, retain, and develop high school and undergraduate students in science, technology, engineering and mathematics (STEM)-related disciplines; and to provide experiences that inspire student interest and achievement in STEM disciplines.

8.11 NASA Student Launch Projects

The NASA Student Launch Projects annually challenges informal organizations and middle school, high school, and college students to design, build, and launch a reusable rocket to one mile above ground level while carrying a scientific or engineering payload. SLP is comprised of two project elements: NASA Student Launch Initiative (SLI) for middle/high school/informal teams and NASA University Student Launch Initiative (USLI) for community college and university teams. USLI is a competition where teams are scored on each element of the project. SLI is not a competition; however, teams must first place in the top of the Team America Rocketry Challenge (TARC) or the Rockets for Schools (R4S) competitions to be eligible to submit a proposal for participation in SLI. Any community college or university located in the United States is eligible to propose to participate in USLI. The challenge of SLP is to design, fabricate, test, and fly a high-powered rocket carrying a science or engineering payload to an altitude of one mile above ground level. Participating students are required to build and maintain a team website; submit and present a series of design reviews to a review panel of NASA engineers, scientists, and educators; and engage other students in hands-on educational activities. Approximately 500 students, educators and mentors participated in SLP in 2011-2012.

8.12 Lunabotics Mining Competition

NASA's Fourth Annual Lunabotics Mining Competition is an international university-level competition designed to engage and retain students in science, technology, engineering and mathematics (STEM). NASA encourages the development of innovative lunar excavation concepts from universities which may result in clever ideas and solutions which could be applied to an actual lunar excavation device or payload. The challenge is for students to design and build an excavator, called a Lunabot, that can mine and deposit a minimum of 10 kilograms of lunar simulant within 10 minutes. The complexities of the challenge include the abrasive characteristics of the BP-1, the weight and size limitations of the Lunabot, and the ability to telerobotically or autonomously control the Lunabot from a remote mission control center. The Lunabots cannot employ any fundamental physical processes (e.g., suction or water cooling in the open lunar environment), gases, fluids, or consumables that would not work in the lunar environment. The scoring for the mining category will require teams to consider a number of design and operation factors such as dust tolerance and projection, communications, vehicle mass, energy/power required, and full autonomy.

To stir innovative technology ideas for excavating lunar soil, a necessary first step toward extracting resources from lunar soil and building bases on the moon, the students are required to design, build, test, and compete a Lunabot. Students compete for monetary awards in seven categories: on-site mining, systems engineering paper, presentation and demonstration, outreach project report, team spirit, and the overall grand prize The Joe Kosmo Award for Excellence. Winners for monetary awards are selected based on numerical scores for each category. Winner of the Joe Kosmo Award for Excellence also receive launch invitations, and travel expenses to a NASA field test. Onsite mining winners also receive launch invitations. There are also several non-monetary award categories including: innovation, social media, and efficient use of communications.

8.13 NASA Tournament Lab

The NASA Tournament Lab (NTL)[54] continued to flourish in FY2012. A few highlights include the development of an Android ECG mobile app with implications for space and third-world medical application; development of several mobile apps that allow planetary observation data to be queried and inspected efficiently and quickly that included a smart app to support educators in the classroom; as well as launching a series of Big Data Challenges in support of the Government's Networking and Information Technology Research and Development (NITRD) Program. NASA worked closely with the National Science Foundation and the Department of Energy on these Big Data challenges. Winners will be formally announced in January 2013.

Unique to the NTL this year was the launch of a video competition to support the 2012 Zero Robotics Challenge. The highest dollar winner of the competition produced a video[55] that during the month of September was one of the top five viral videos.

The NTL ends this successful year preparing to launch a challenge for the International Space Station (ISS) Program. The ISS Longeron Shadowing challenge will be a series of contests designed to bring a unique approach to determining if NASA can optimize power production from the solar arrays.

8.14 NASA Innovation Pavilion

Another significant milestone is that NASA is once again up and running with challenges on its InnoCentive Innovation Pavilion.[56] As FY2012 concluded, the Langley Research Center was putting the wraps on a theoretical challenge to find a new method to measure the strain on Kevlar and Vectran straps in the 25 to 125°C range to advance techniques for use in inflatable habitation structures. Fy2013 will bring the posting of a challenge to help find a device capable of measuring intracranial pressure in spaceflight to support research seeking ways to mitigate vision changes in astronauts. This challenge is unique in that NASA used its internal crowdsourcing tool, NASA@work as the starting point to gather information internal to NASA as well as using its technology scouting platform (yet2.com) to seek unique sources of understanding what technologies may be out there that meet a more mature technology readiness level. Launching the challenge on the Innovation Pavilion will lend yet another source of advancing research in a key focus area of human health and performance in space. The CoECI will be monitoring the results this next year with a keen focus on the lessons learned that result from this multi-platform approach.

---

[54] http://community.topcoder.com/ntl/
[55] http://tongal.com/project/ZeroRobotics
[56] https://www.innocentive.com/pavilion/NASA

9. National Institute of Standards and Technology

9.1 NIST SHA-3 Hash Competition

In order to strengthen and ensure future information security NIST challenged the global cryptographic community to come up with a new cryptographic hash algorithm, SHA-3. Hash algorithms are used in numerous everyday transactions to authenticate and protect information. This major challenge allowed the NIST's Computer Security Division to tap into the best cryptography talent from around the world to help solve this critical challenge with the winners receiving the scientific and commercial recognition of being among the elite in their field. In addition to identifying the best SHA-3 algorithm, this competition has contributed to tremendous gains in the cryptography community regarding the general theory and understanding of hash algorithms, far beyond what NIST could have accomplished alone.

A cryptographic hash algorithm is one of the fundamental tools of modern information security. It is a widely used tool that creates a "fingerprint" or a "message digest" of a file, message, or block of data that can be used for digital signatures, message authentication codes, and many other security applications in the information infrastructure. Following attacks that broke existing hash algorithms, in 2007 NIST decided that it was prudent to develop a new hash algorithm to augment and revise the Federal Information Processing Standard (FIPS) 180–2, which specifies hash algorithms for Federal use and is widely adopted by the IT industry. The new hash algorithm would be referred to as "SHA–3", and would be developed through a public competition. NIST intended that SHA–3 would specify an unclassified, publicly disclosed algorithm(s), which would be available worldwide without royalties or other intellectual property restrictions, and would be capable of protecting sensitive information for decades. The worldwide cryptographic community provided an enormous amount of feedback throughout the competition. Most of the comments were sent to NIST and a public hash forum. in addition, many of the cryptanalysis and performance studies were published as papers in major cryptographic conferences or leading cryptographic journals. NIST also hosted three SHA-3 candidate conferences to obtain public feedback.

Based on the public comments and internal review of the candidates, NIST announced Keccak as the winner of the SHA-3 Cryptographic Hash Algorithm Competition on October 2, 2012, and ended the five-year competition. The Keccak algorithm was created by Guido Bertoni, Joan Daemen and Gilles Van Assche of STMicroelectronics and Michael Peeters of NXP Semiconductors. Per the terms of the competition, SHA-3 will remain an unclassified, publicly disclosed algorithm available worldwide on a royalty free basis as a new security tool for network system designers.

10. Department of Defense

10.1 Army Challenge: Federal Virtual Worlds Challenge

The U.S. Army Sergeant First Class Paul Ray Smith Simulation and Training Technology Center of the Human Research and Engineering Directorate, U.S. Army Research Laboratory introduced the inaugural Federal Virtual Worlds Challenges (FVWC) in the summer of 2009 to reach a global research and developmental community.[57] The goal was to explore a multitude of potential capabilities and developments within virtual environments. The demonstrated benefit of that first challenge to research in immersive environments resulted in the approval from the Office of the Assistant Secretary of the Army for Acquisition, Logistics, and Technology for the continuation of FVWC as an annual event.

Following the Defense GameTech User's Conference, winners had the opportunity to describe their solutions to USG users and policymakers during a panel session at the Federal Consortium of Virtual Worlds Conference. Some entries were already USG-developed projects that benefitted from further socialization and reuse within the industry. Various finalists built relationships with one another leading to working partnerships. Finalists included the Challenge results on resumes, product advertisements, and corporate achievements as a demonstration of expertise in the field.

The Challenge was divided into two focus areas: 'Engaging Learning Strategies' and the 'Holodeck – Making It So'.

The Engaging Learning Strategies Focus Area – This focus area was a call for demonstrations of learning activities in virtual environments that depict effective strategies to engage learners. When entries were received in this focus area, they logically fell into three categories: Concept Building, Distributed Learning and Familiarization. A description of the finalists in each category follows.

In the Concept Building Category which included entries focused on presenting learning tasks in an immersive environment, the Grand Prize and First Place Winner was "Interactive Graphic Novel Approach to Guided Learning. This battle care trainer demonstrates how basic battlefield trauma triage could be trained using interactive interface techniques provided on the iPad. In BattleCare, the learner plays the role of Airman Collins, who is the medic on duty in Gardez near the Afghanistan border. The

---

[57] All DOD prize summaries here are excerpted from the March 2013 Report from the Department of Defense Office of the Assistant Secretary of Defense for Acquisition, Technology, and Logistics to Congress on the Prizes for Advanced Technology Achievements Under Title 10, United States Code, Section 2374a.

learner, as Airman Collins, learns the basics of A-B-C – checking for Airway, Breathing and Circulation in a trauma patient. His mentor, Sergeant Rodriguez, allows Collins to make his own choices (Discovery Learning) but provides feedback on those choices (Guided Discovery). The episode begins with the arrival of the trauma case and ends with successful stabilization and helicopter evacuation of the patient. The rendering style, character positioning, and page layout is based on graphic novel conventions. Gesture-based interaction makes the learner feel like they are touching the patient. Exploration gives a sense of game play while the mentor's guidance means that the learner does not get lose. Additional information on this entry can be found at http://www.clinispace.com/fvwc/Engaging Learning.html.

Distributed Learning Category - The Distributed Learning entries demonstrated instruction available to groups that supported collaboration and/or providing a distributed learning platform.

First Place Winner: Creative Learning in a Wet Lab – This entry was developed to support small communities spread across the Alaskan Bush, some of which have no road access, to overcome a lack of infrastructure and trained lab assistants needed to provide a high quality, real time science lab. The virtual wet lab system provides a virtual "hands-on" lab environment where students can do a live lab together, regardless of physical location. Intuitive camera presets ease the frustration of trying to examine multiple objects in real time in order to complete labs in faster than real time. One lab allows students to instantly cross fruit fly traits and explore the fundamentals of Mendelian genetics. Another lab examines the DNA of a poached fish as students complete a 24 hour lab in 2 hours. A virtual world is used to re-conceptualize what it means to conduct a science lab: the student becomes a participant within whatever image or data they are observing. For example, by controlling time, students experience predatory natural selection as a bird hunting for food during 250 years of environmental change. Other labs, such as fermentation and biochemical evidence for evolution, delay reactions to enhance data collection. Students interact with altered time and virtual space as they develop essential lab skills that can be applied toward new situations in more advanced classes. Additional information on this entry can be found at http://www.pwscc.edu/academics/creative-learning-in-a-virtual-wet-lab/

Familiarization Category - The Familiarization category provided an immersive environment for learners to become familiar with physical spaces or to link concepts to physical spaces.

First Place Winner: United States Air Force Academy Browser Based 3D Virtual Campus Tour - The United States Air Force Academy (USAFA), located in Colorado Springs, Colorado, found that travel limitations hindered their ability to recruit potential cadets. They wanted an effective recruitment method that would eliminate inconvenience to these potential cadets or their families. USAFA found that virtual worlds could offer the ability to have a 3D virtual campus where potential cadets could walk around and learn about culture, size, and beauty of the campus through an avatar. This immersive 3D virtual campus tour allows students to access the campus quickly and easily using a URL through any major browser. Potential cadets have the ability to tour the campus on their own, or can attend individual or group tours with an automated admissions representative who is able to showcase all of the Academy's features. Non-playing characters provide additional information on what the Academy has to offer. Interactive games such as basketball, hockey, parachute and a flight simulator offer a fun and engaging medium to keep cadets coming back to learn more. Points from trivia and games allow for the purchase of USAFA branded virtual apparel and accessories, including the top prize - the mascot uniform. Then cadets are able to access the application quickly and easily through the virtual campus tour once they have decided USAFA is the right place for them. The development of the 3D virtual campus tour MMO for the USAFA has proven to be a valued addition to the recruitment process with over 1,000 potential cadets in the system within the first few months. Additional information on this entry can be found at http://www.designingdigitaHv.com/portfolio/virtual-worlds/united-states-air-force-academv-browserbased-3d-virtual-campus-tour.

The 'Holodeck - Making It So' Focus Area - This focus area was a call to developers to make significant advancements toward reducing the gap between the player and the environment using low cost materials. Entries were limited to $600 hardware costs (aside from the computing platform) each.

Grand Prize and First Place Winner: CyberSim Holodeck - This entry uses two scenarios to demonstrate the potential capabilities of various virtual world input devices: microphone, keyboard, Xbox Kinect, and the Emotiv brain computer interface head set. Each of the devices was made compatible with SecondLife and OpenSim and was an Augmented Virtual Reality tool that brought real world experiences into Virtual Worlds. The CyberSim Holodeck models a Security Operations Center (SOC) as an augmented virtual cyber security analyst workspace. The CyberSim Holodeck combines virtual reality (SecondLife and Military Open Simulator Enterprise Strategy (MOSES)) with augmented reality technologies (Smartphone and HTML5 viewer) to create an analytic training environment for the next generation cyber security analyst using low-cost non-traditional input devices. Examples of input devices include a microphone for Voice Recognition/Command using PocketPhinx software; a standard keyboard for Text to Speech using cepstral and flite software; an Xbox Kinect for skeletal tracking using OpenNI and FAAST software, and an Emotiv head set for EGG using Expressive, Affective, Cognitive Suites. Augmented Reality capabilities were demonstrated, using smartphone applications, further reducing the gap between the player and environment to bring real experiences into the Holodeck virtual environment. Additional information on this entry can be found at http://www.cvbersim.net/Holodeck/Holodeck.php

10.2 Air Force Challenges: Fuel Scrubber, Grey DATA, Durable Dielectrics on Polycarbonate, and Energetic Core-Shell Nanocluster Production

In FY 2012, the Air Force Research Laboratory (AFRL) executed four award challenges to address near-term problems facing the Warfighter. By opening these challenges up to the world through InnoCentive, AFRL was able to increase the number of people addressing this problem by over 100 fold and received workable solutions within a very short amount of time.

The primary goal of the Air Force (AF) challenge program is to apply emerging and existing technologies in novel ways to solve near-term problems facing the Warfighter. One of the challenges in meeting these urgent needs is the long timeline associated with establishing a program to execute such a solution, which is largely a result of established business and acquisition processes for funding allocation, market surveys, contracting, program management, and review that are tuned for longer term research activities. Each challenge was assigned a Challenge Owner from a technical directorate that had responsibility in the area of interest. If a challenge produced a usable result, the award was paid and the Challenge Owner would incorporate the result in their technology development program. The four challenges and results are as follows:

10.2.1 Fuel Recovery: This theoretical challenge was to create a system that could enable recovery of Air Force Jet engine fuel spilled from a storage silo. The system must remove synthetic surfactants that are commonly used in firefighting foams as well as water and other debris. The solution needs to be portable as part of an overall fuel recovery solution that would be able to recover up to 200,000 gallons in an 8 hour period allowing the fuel to be immediately ready for use in operational aircraft. There were 447 people that responded to this challenge and showed interest in providing solutions. Of the 17 concepts that were submitted, three solutions had merit and were worth pursuing. Two of these ideas solved one of the requirements for Joint Capability Technology Demonstration (JCTD) program. The JCTD program manager decided to make a dual award and pursue two of these ideas to reduce the technology risk to his program. The JCTD program manager is now developing working prototypes for both concepts to find out which one will work better in the field environments. Prior to the challenge, the program manager had no viable ideas on how to solve this problem.

10.2.2 Grey Data: AF researchers routinely process large amounts of information from diverse sources (e.g., sensors, social media, public records). Data on people's activities and habits are increasingly available online, raising the possibility of a researcher inadvertently violating privacy act laws. This ideation challenge was to find a trustworthy automated mechanism to determine whether online information is public or private. There were 684 people that responded to this challenge, and the ideas that were submitted identified many partial solutions that could be combined to create a robust automated discovery mechanism. It also identified new data mining software that the researchers were not aware of (e.g., "Splunk") that could be trained to alert on private data. The results of this challenge were added to a legal studies report produced by the USAF Academy on how to determine boundaries of social media research.

10.2.3 Durable Dielectrics on Polycarbonate: AF researchers were looking for a dielectric coating and a process to apply it to a curved polycarbonate substrate whose surface area ranges from 150 to 750 square cm. The coating had to act as a "hot mirror" (transmit visible, reflect near infra-red), be up to 10 microns in thickness, and maintain its integrity and performance under environmental conditions (-40 C to +70 C, and 0% to 98% RH, Mil Std Salt fog testing). Although 237 people participated in this challenge, there was no viable solution found and no award was made.

10.2.4 Energetic Core-Shell Nanocluster Production: AF researchers were looking for material processing technologies for the production of core-shell nanoclusters of energetic materials with particle diameters between 5 and 25 nm. Emphasis was on a controllable process that produced air-stable, consistent particles at increased rates that could scale up to at least lg/hour. This challenge had 202 participants but the challenge was also sent to over 100 different nano-research centers across the United States with information about this challenge and AFRL's interest in following up with a Small Business Research effort to test out a potential solution. This challenge is still under evaluation from those responses submitted to the Challenge. AFRL was also contacted by one credible source that did not want to submit to the prize but indicated that they would be submitting to the SBIR solicitation in order to retain control of their Intellectual Property and noted that they would not have responded to the SBIR announcement without first being alerted to it by the challenge.

10.3 DARPA Challenges: Cash for Locating and Identifying Quick Response

In FY 2012, DARPA executed two challenge award programs: (1) the Cash for Locating and Identifying Quick Response (CLIQR) Codes Quest Challenge, and (2) the Shredder Challenge.

10.3.1 CLIQR Codes Quest: The CLIQR Challenge sought to advance the understanding of social media and the Internet to explore the role each plays in timely communication, wide-area team building, and urgent mobilization required to solve broad-scope, time-critical problems. The DARPA CLIQR Quest Challenge provided an increased understanding of how social networks organize around a common theme. The hypothesis was that information brokers would emerge in the development of a network and could be identified through nodal analysis of activity. The Challenge demonstrated that social networks formed as hypothesized, enabling DARPA to map and analyze the process through a semi-controlled scenario. Subsequent to the event, DARPA discussed the results, methods employed, and potential ramifications with several organizations including PeopleBrowsr, HHS ASPR, and the Department of Homeland Security Office of Resilience Policy. In addition, all four Services received information regarding and had exposure to this Challenge. The DARPA CLIQR Quest Challenge achieved its goals and has helped DARPA advance the understanding of social media and the Internet and explored the role the Internet and social networking play in the timely communication, wide area team-building, and urgent mobilization required to solve broad scope, time-critical problems.

10.3.2 Shredder Challenge: The DARPA Shredder Challenge called upon participants to piece together a series of shredded documents using any means available, including manual methods, computerized methods, and crowd sourcing. Five one-sided handwritten documents were shredded into more than 10,000 pieces, and the images of the shredded pieces were posted online. Document subject matter and the degree of shredding were varied to present problems of increasing difficulty. To complete each problem, participants provided answers to questions embedded in the content of reconstructed documents, with the intent of mirroring the problem facing an intelligence analyst with a similar task. Competitors were awarded points according to an established rubric for successfully reconstructing documents and to a sufficient degree that they could answer embedded questions. The goal of the DARPA Shredder Challenge was to accelerate technological solutions and problem-solving techniques enabling the reconstruction of shredded documents at the tactical edge. Specifically, the program goals were to: (1) identify and assess potential capabilities that could be used by warfighters to more quickly obtain valuable information from confiscated, shredded documents, and (2) gain a quantitative understanding of potential vulnerabilities inherent to the shredding of sensitive U.S. National Security documents.

The DARPA Shredder Challenge was a successful demonstration of the potential of an integrated human-machine approach to solve large, complex problems that would be near impossible by any other means. DARPA discussed the results with several organizations within the law enforcement, military, and intelligence communities including the Federal Bureau of Investigation Questioned Documents Unit, Army G2 Document and Media Exploitation, and Sandia National Laboratories. The DARPA Shredder Challenge achieved its goals and stimulated interest in the programs and projects of interest to the DOD science and technology community. The event attracted a large pool of nontraditional participants. The varied methods used have potential implications for problems generally considered unsolvable by conventional means. This result promises to inspire a new class of problem solving approaches in areas important to National Security.

www.ingramcontent.com/pod-product-compliance
Lightning Source LLC
Chambersburg PA
CBHW080316290526
45790CB00005B/2065